DELUXE
GUITAR
PLAY-ALONG

AUDIO ACCESS INCLUDED

TOP ROCK HITS

T0057727

PLAYBACK+
Speed • Pitch • Balance • Loop

To access audio visit:
www.halleonard.com/mylibrary

Enter Code
4282-8072-7618-8670

ISBN 978-1-5400-0312-6

HAL•LEONARD®

7777 W. BLUEMOUND RD. P.O. BOX 13819 MILWAUKEE, WI 53213

For all works contained herein:
Unauthorized copying, arranging, adapting, recording, Internet posting, public performance,
or other distribution of the printed or recorded music in this publication is an infringement of copyright.
Infringers are liable under the law.

Visit Hal Leonard Online at
www.halleonard.com

GUITAR NOTATION LEGEND

THE MUSICAL STAFF shows pitches and rhythms and is divided by bar lines into measures. Pitches are named after the first seven letters of the alphabet.

TABLATURE graphically represents the guitar fingerboard. Each horizontal line represents a string, and each number represents a fret.

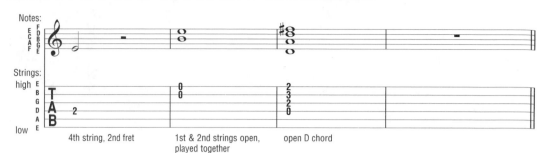

4th string, 2nd fret   1st & 2nd strings open, played together   open D chord

HALF-STEP BEND: Strike the note and bend up 1/2 step.

WHOLE-STEP BEND: Strike the note and bend up one step.

GRACE NOTE BEND: Strike the note and immediately bend up as indicated.

SLIGHT (MICROTONE) BEND: Strike the note and bend up 1/4 step.

BEND AND RELEASE: Strike the note and bend up as indicated, then release back to the original note. Only the first note is struck.

PRE-BEND: Bend the note as indicated, then strike it.

VIBRATO: The string is vibrated by rapidly bending and releasing the note with the fretting hand.

PALM MUTING: The note is partially muted by the pick hand lightly touching the string(s) just before the bridge.

HAMMER-ON: Strike the first (lower) note with one finger, then sound the higher note (on the same string) with another finger by fretting it without picking.

PULL-OFF: Place both fingers on the notes to be sounded. Strike the first note and without picking, pull the finger off to sound the second (lower) note.

LEGATO SLIDE: Strike the first note and then slide the same fret-hand finger up or down to the second note. The second note is not struck.

SHIFT SLIDE: Same as legato slide, except the second note is struck.

TRILL: Very rapidly alternate between the notes indicated by continuously hammering on and pulling off.

TAPPING: Hammer ("tap") the fret indicated with the pick-hand index or middle finger and pull off to the note fretted by the fret hand.

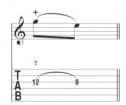

NATURAL HARMONIC: Strike the note while the fret-hand lightly touches the string directly over the fret indicated.

PINCH HARMONIC: The note is fretted normally and a harmonic is produced by adding the edge of the thumb or the tip of the index finger of the pick hand to the normal pick attack.

TREMOLO PICKING: The note is picked as rapidly and continuously as possible.

VIBRATO BAR DIVE AND RETURN: The pitch of the note or chord is dropped a specified number of steps (in rhythm), then returned to the original pitch.

VIBRATO BAR SCOOP: Depress the bar just before striking the note, then quickly release the bar.

VIBRATO BAR DIP: Strike the note and then immediately drop a specified number of steps, then release back to the original pitch.

Additional Musical Definitions

(accent)

- Accentuate note (play it louder).

(staccato)

- Play the note short.

D.S. al Coda

- Go back to the sign (%), then play until the measure marked "*To Coda*," then skip to the section labelled "**Coda**."

D.C. al Fine

- Go back to the beginning of the song and play until the measure marked "*Fine*" (end).

Fill

- Label used to identify a brief melodic figure which is to be inserted into the arrangement.

N.C.

- Harmony is implied.

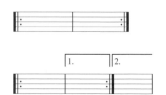

- Repeat measures between signs.

- When a repeated section has different endings, play the first ending only the first time and the second ending only the second time.

TOP ROCK HITS

Basket Case

Words by Billie Joe
Music by Green Day

Tune down 1/2 step:
(low to high) Eb-Ab-Db-Gb-Bb-Eb

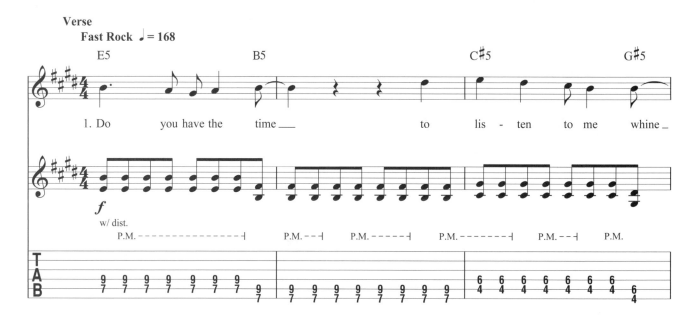

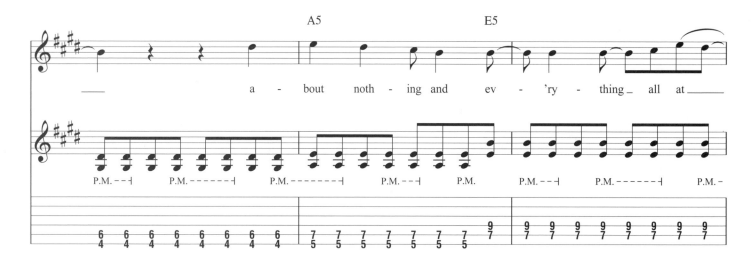

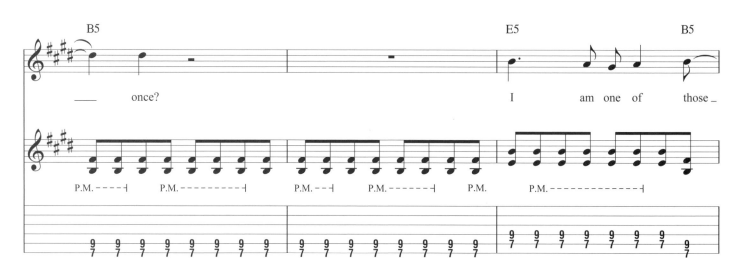

© 1994 WB MUSIC CORP. and GREEN DAZE MUSIC
All Rights Administered by WB MUSIC CORP.
All Rights Reserved   Used by Permission

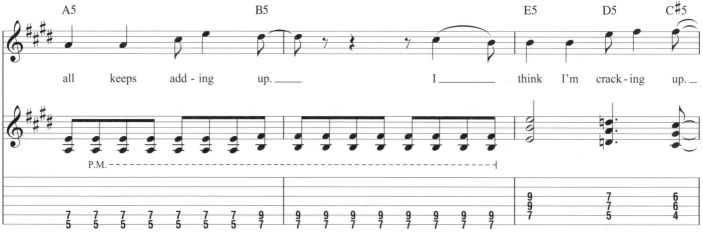

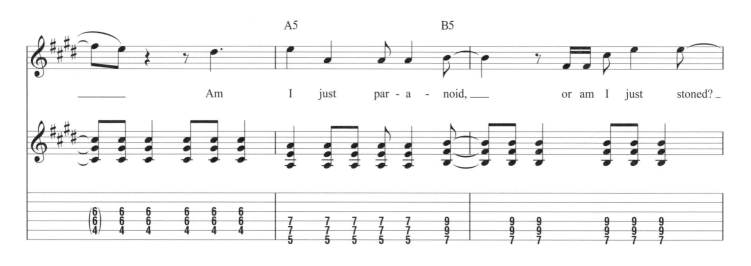

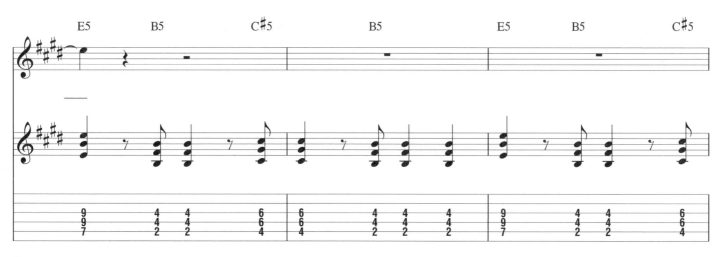

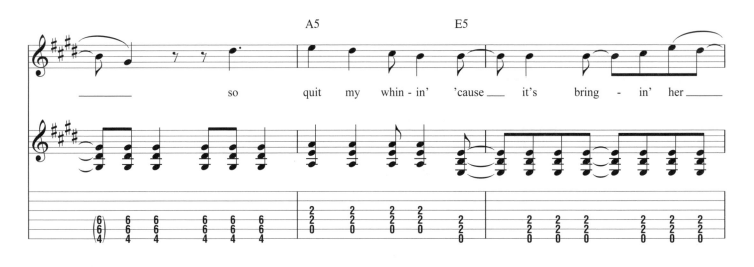

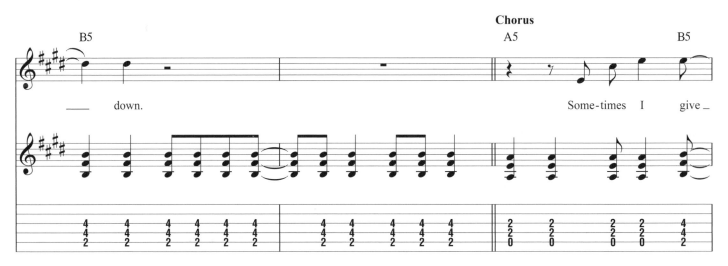

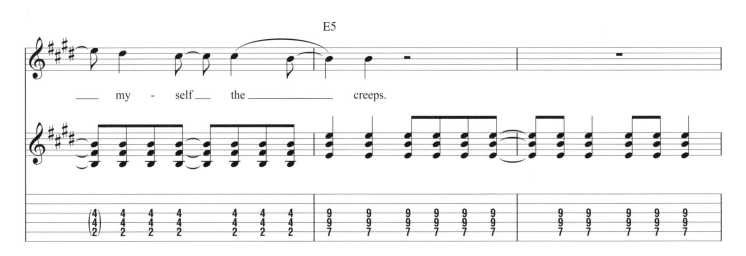

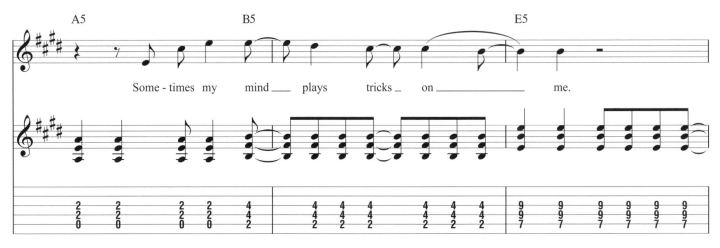

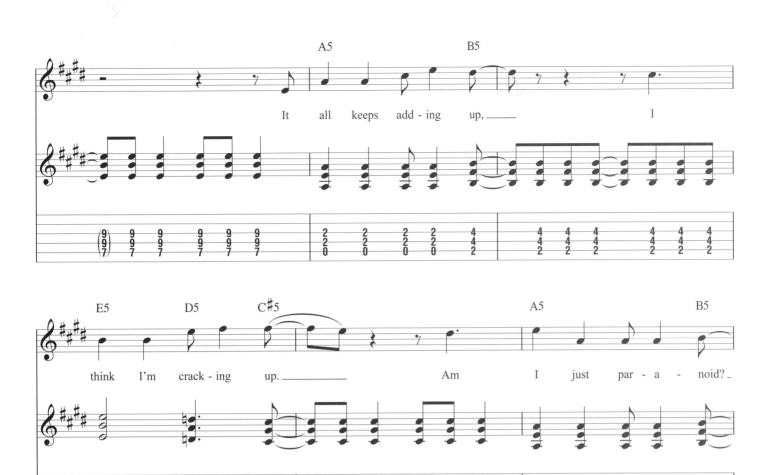

Interlude

so I bet-ter hold _____ on. _____

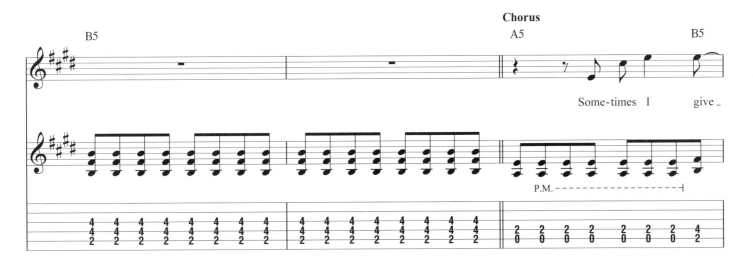

Chorus

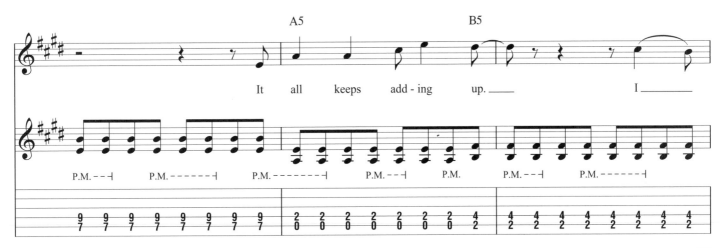

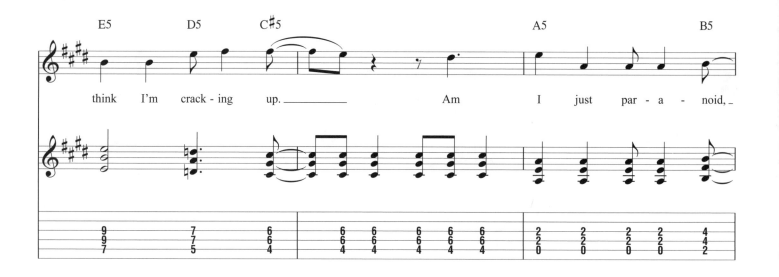

think I'm crack-ing up. _____ Am I just par-a-noid, _

Outro

_ or am I just stoned? _____

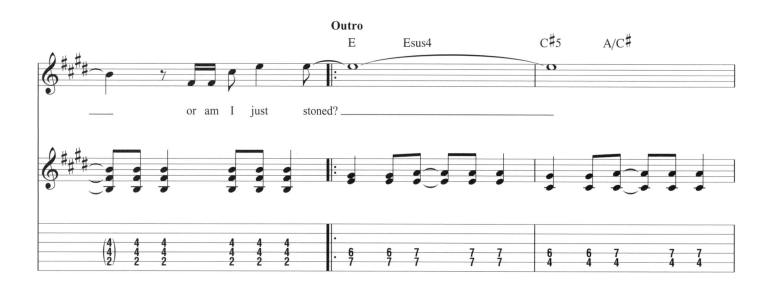

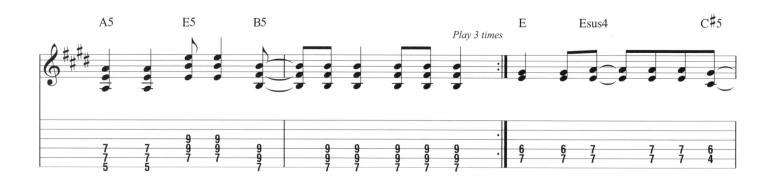

Play 3 times

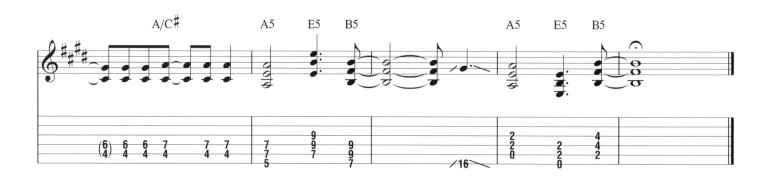

Black Hole Sun

Words and Music by Chris Cornell

Drop D tuning:
(low to high) D-A-D-G-B-E

Intro
Slow Rock ♩ = 52

w/ clean tone
let ring throughout

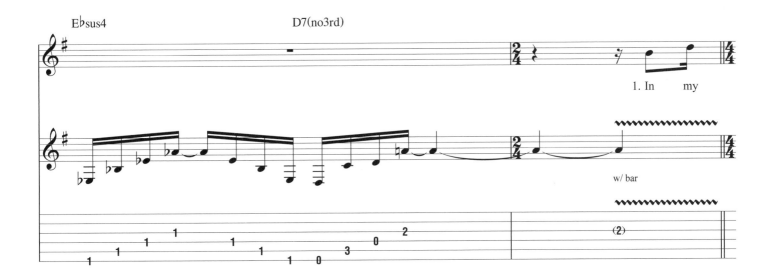

1. In my

Verse

eyes, in-dis-posed, in dis-guise as no___ one knows,___ hides the face,___
2. *See additional lyrics*

w/ Leslie effect
2nd time, dist. off

Copyright © 1994 You Make Me Sick I Make Music
All Rights Administered by BMG Rights Management (US) LLC
All Rights Reserved   Used by Permission

Chorus

14

wash a - way __ the rain? _____ Black hole __ sun, __ won't you come? __ Won't __ you come? __

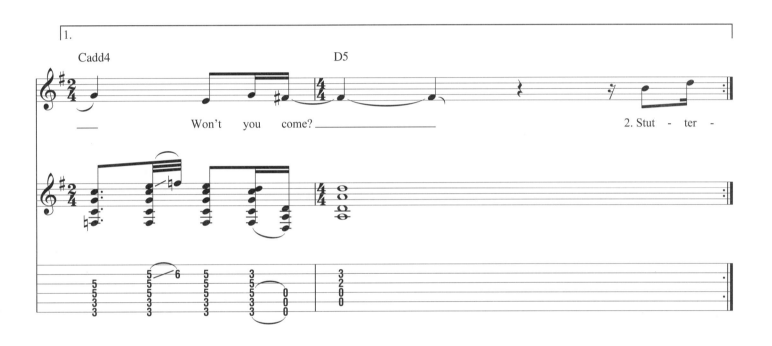

1.

Won't you come? _____ 2. Stut - ter -

2.

_____ Black hole __ sun, __ won't you come __ and

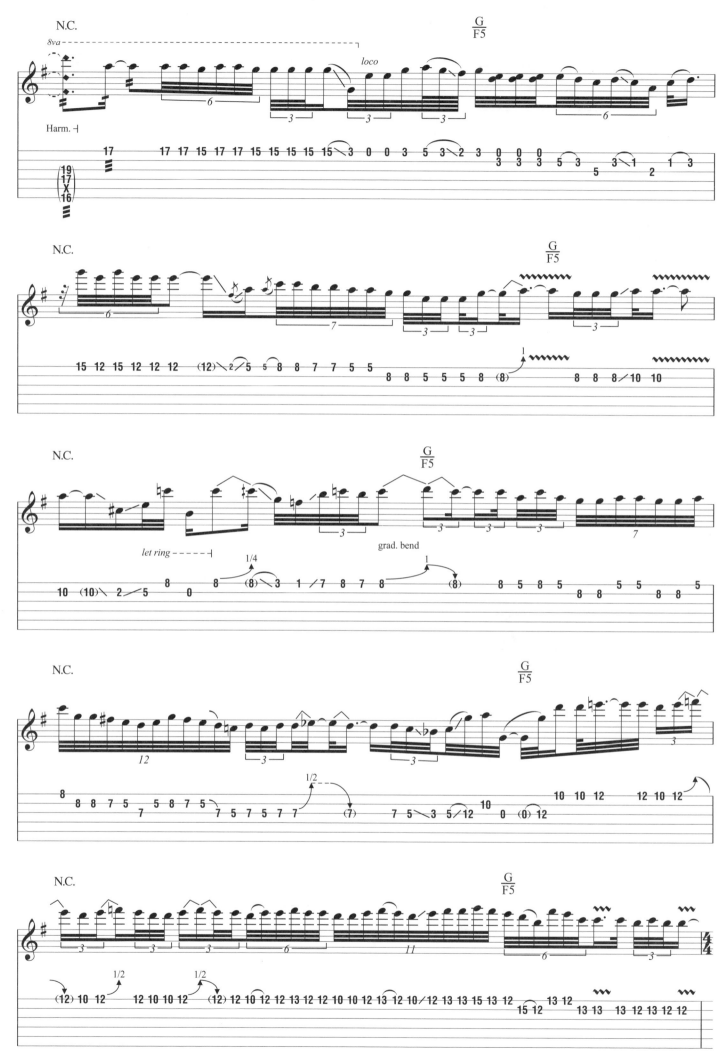

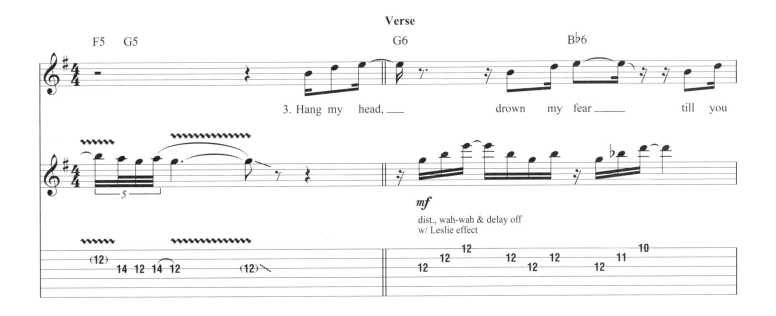

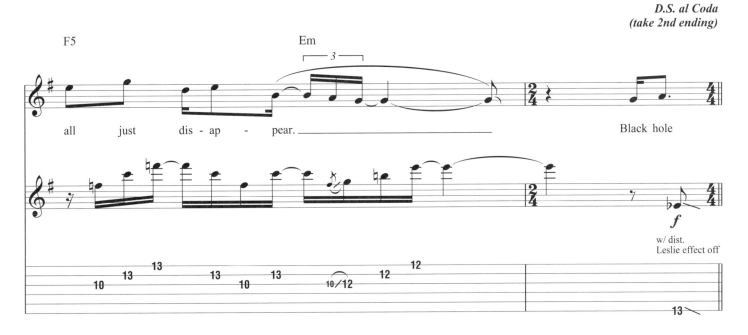

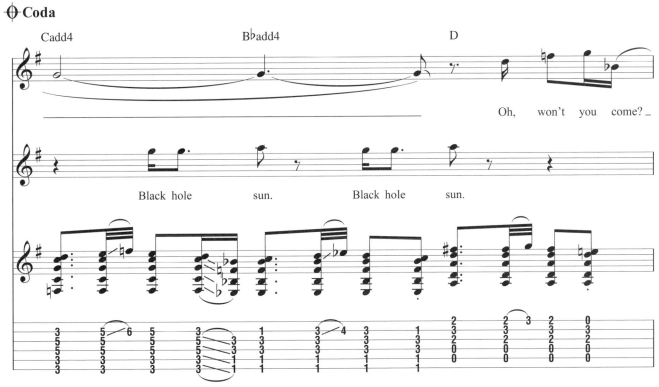

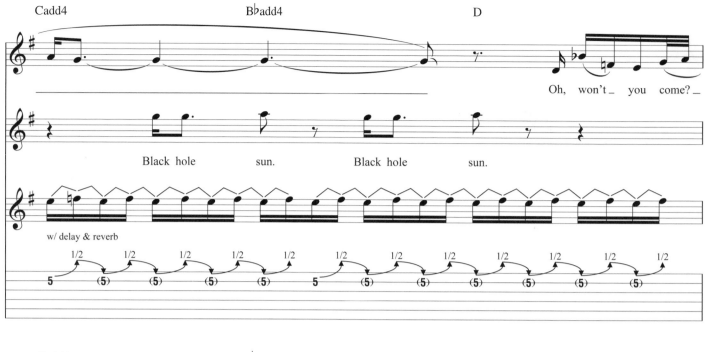

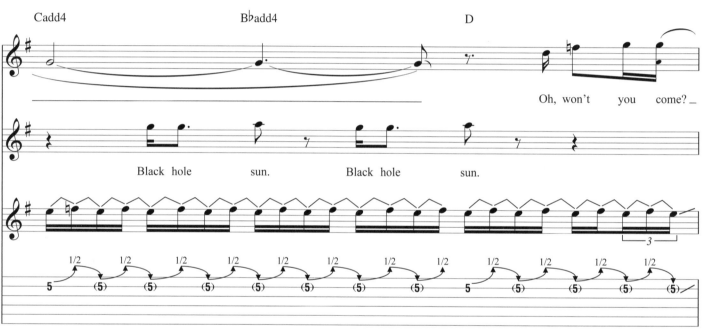

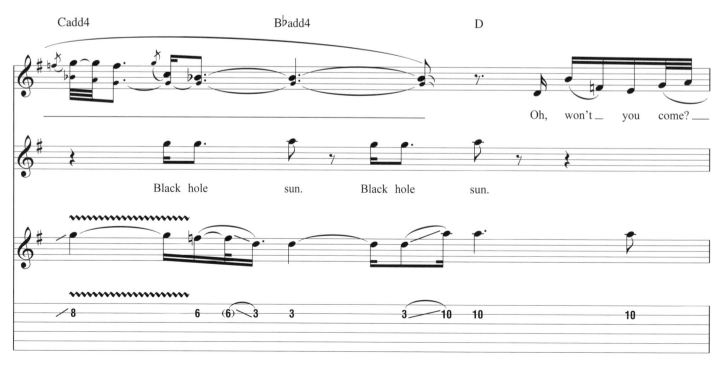

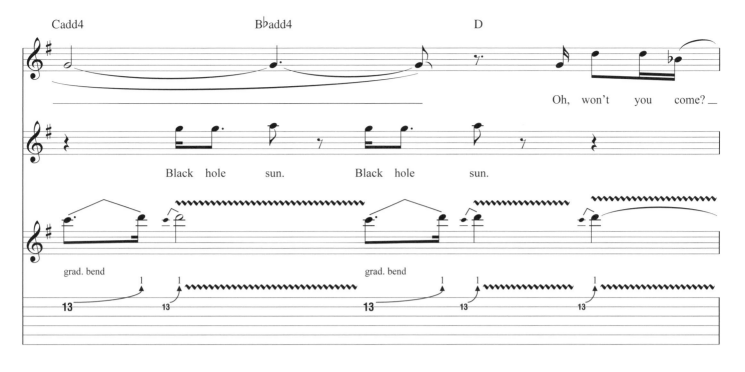

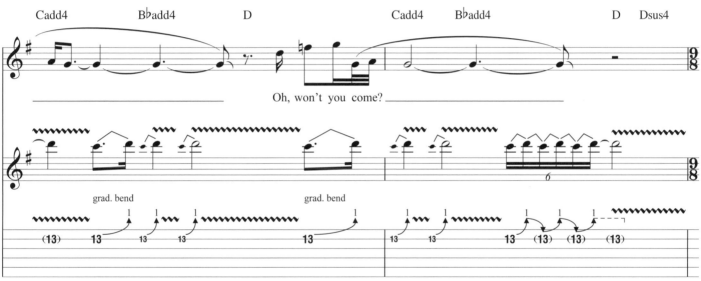

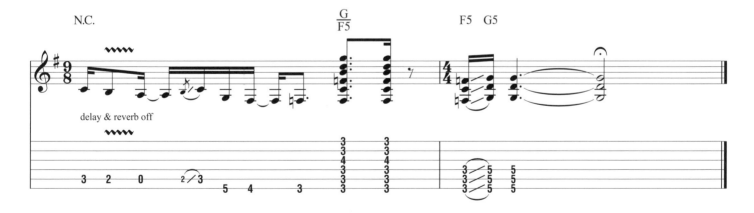

Additional Lyrics

2. Stuttering, cold and damp.
  Steal the warm wind, tired friend.
  Times are gone for honest men,
  And sometimes far too long for snakes.
  In my shoes, a walking sleep.
  In my youth I pray to keep.
  Heaven send hell away.
  No one sings like you anymore.

Come As You Are

Words and Music by Kurt Cobain

Tune down one step:
(low to high) D-G-C-F-A-D

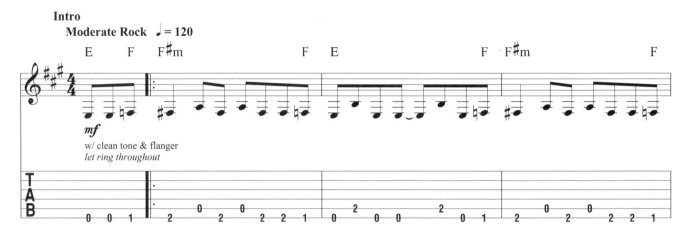

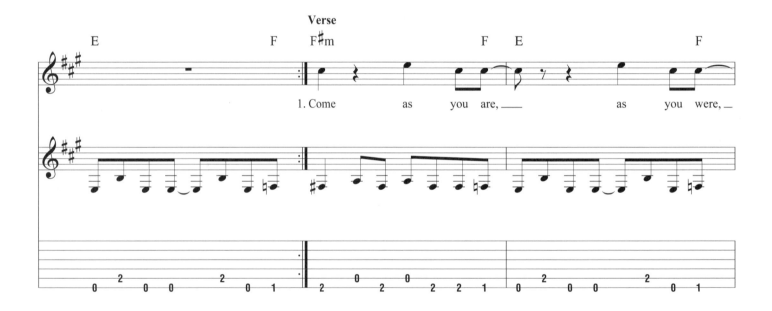

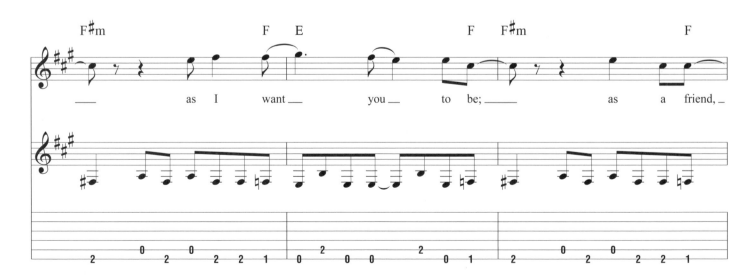

Copyright © 1991 The End Of Music and Primary Wave Tunes
All Rights Administered by BMG Rights Management (US) LLC
All Rights Reserved   Used by Permission

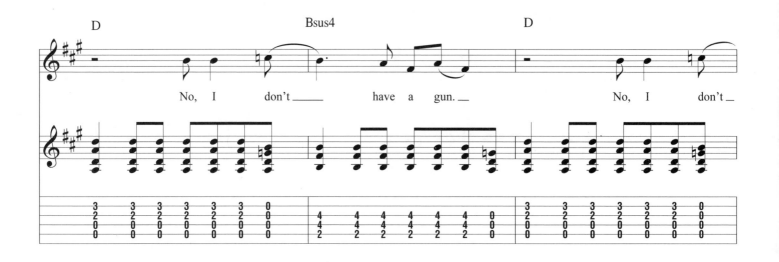

No, I don't _____ have a gun. _____ No, I don't _____

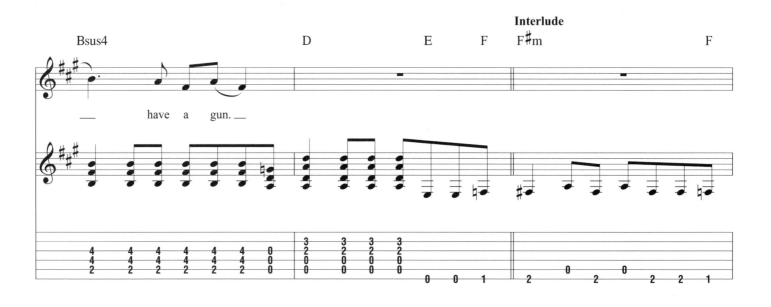

_____ have a gun. _____

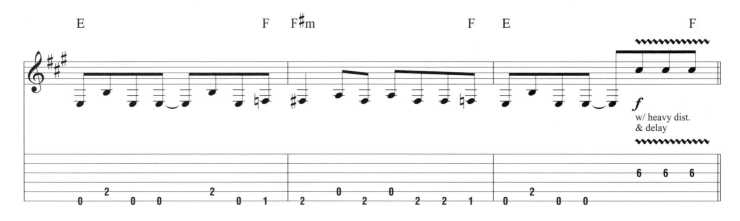

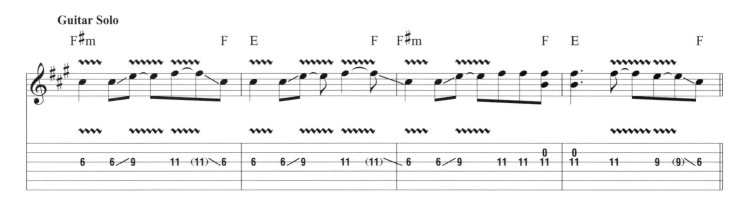

Do I Wanna Know?

Words and Music by Alex Turner

Copyright © 2013 EMI Music Publishing Ltd.
All Rights Administered by Sony/ATV Music Publishing LLC, 424 Church Street, Suite 1200, Nashville, TN 37219
International Copyright Secured   All Rights Reserved

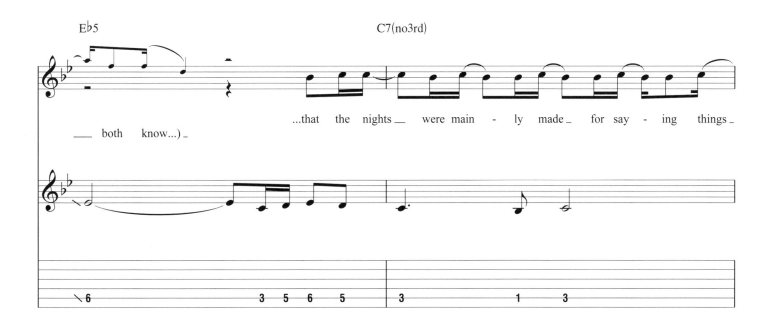

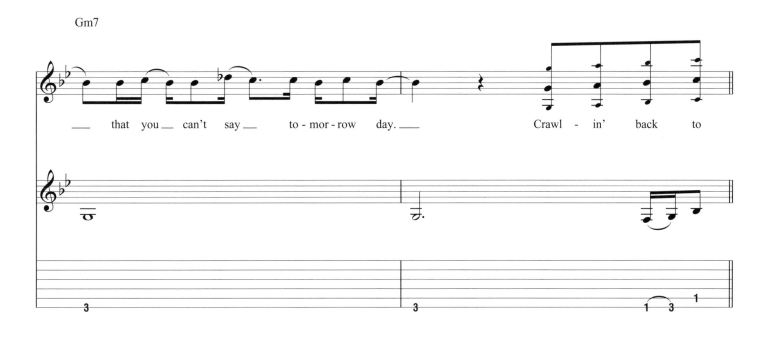

do. May-be I'm too bus-y be-ing yours to fall for some-

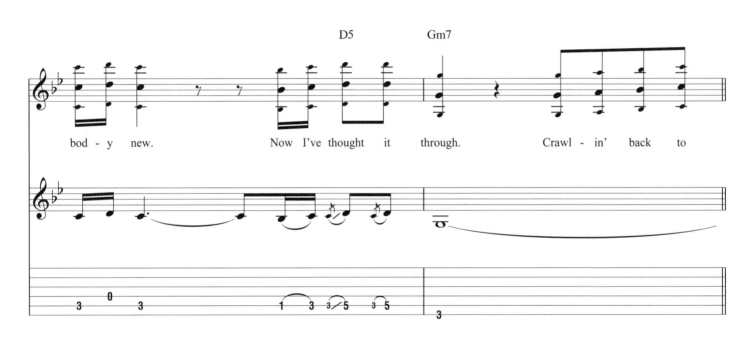

bod-y new. Now I've thought it through. Crawl-in' back to

Verse

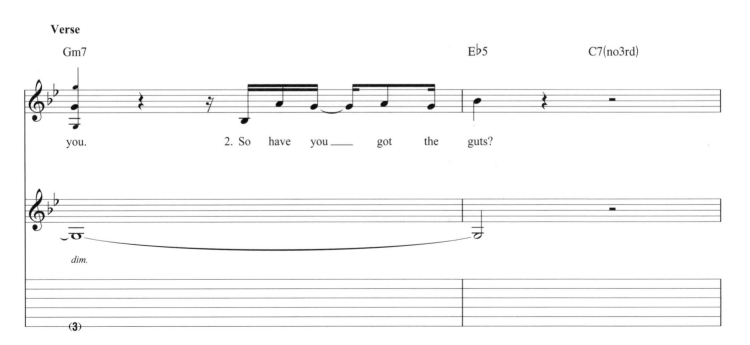

you. 2. So have you ___ got the guts?

dim.

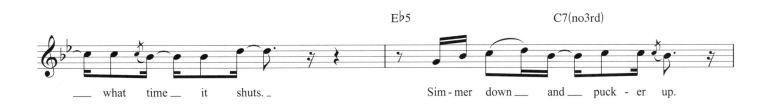

Gtr. tacet

Been won - d'ring if___ your heart's___ still o - pen, and___ if so___ I wan - na know___

___ what time___ it shuts.___ Sim - mer down___ and___ puck - er up.

D5　　　　Gm7

I'm sor - ry to in - ter - rupt,___ it's just,___ I'm con - stant - ly on the cusp of___

___ try - ing to kiss___ you,___ I don't know if___

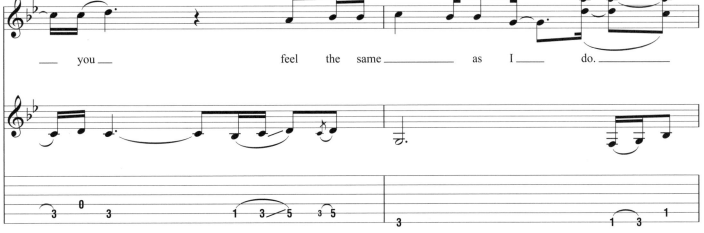

___ you ___ feel the same ___ as I ___ do. ___

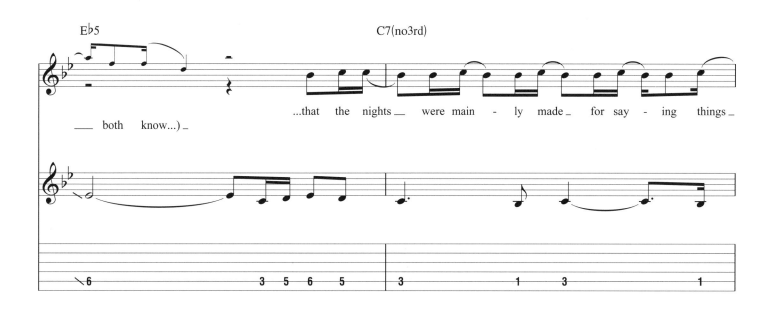

...that the nights ___ were main - ly made ___ for say - ing things ___

___ both know...) ___

___ that you ___ can't say ___ to-mor-row day. ___

Crawl - in' back to

Chorus

you.   Ev - er thought of call - ing when ___ you've had a few?   'Cause I al - ways

(Crawl - in' back to   you.   You've had a few. ___

Gold on the Ceiling

Words and Music by Dan Auerbach, Patrick Carney and Brian Burton

Copyright © 2011 McMoore McLesst Publishing (BMI) and Sweet Science (ASCAP)
All Rights on behalf of McMoore McLesst Publishing in the world excluding Australia and New Zealand Administered by Wixen Music Publishing, Inc.
All Rights on behalf of McMoore McLesst Publishing in Australia and New Zealand Administered by GaGa Music
All Rights Reserved   Used by Permission

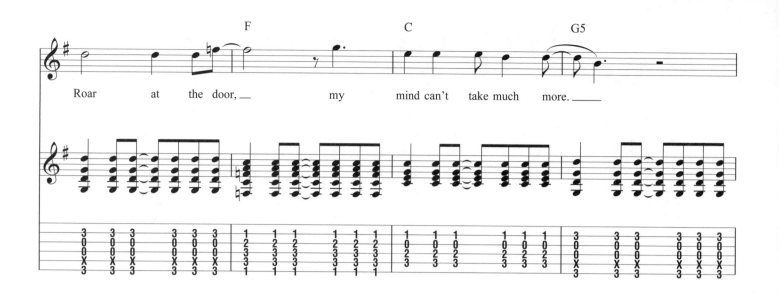

Roar at the door, ___ my mind can't take much more. ___

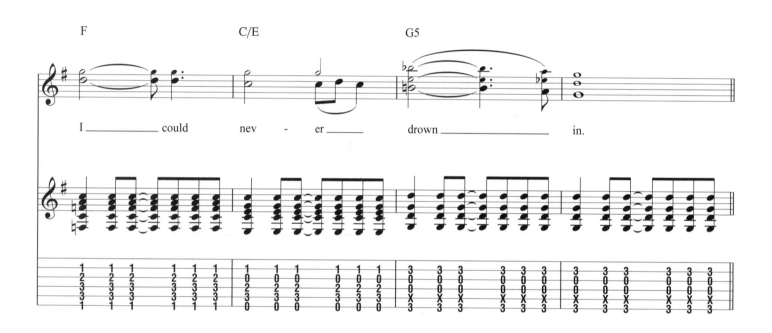

I ___ could nev - er ___ drown ___ in.

𝄋 Pre-Chorus

N.C.

They wan-na get my,

w/ dist.

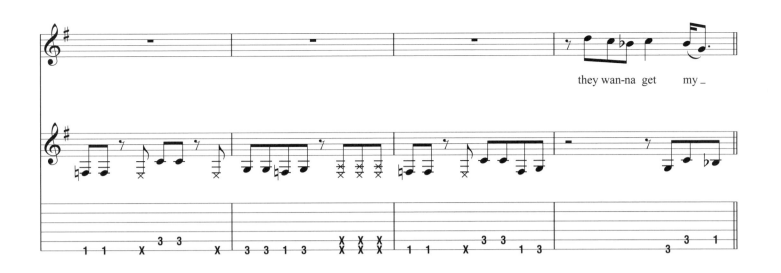

they wan-na get my ___

Chorus

gold   on   the ceil - ing.   I ain't blind;   it's just   a mat - ter of

slight P.M. -----

To Coda ⊕

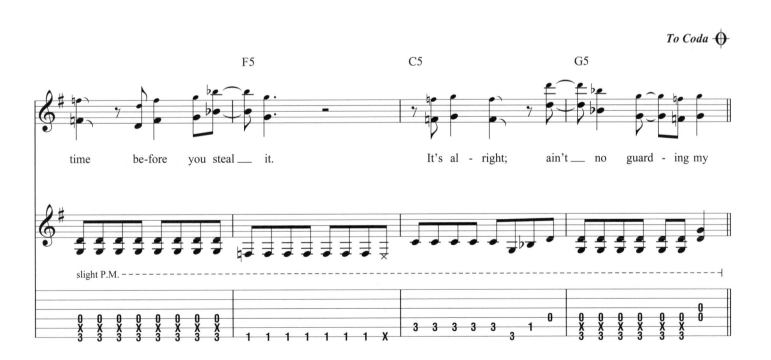

time   be-fore   you steal ___ it.   It's al - right;   ain't ___ no   guard - ing my

slight P.M. -----

Guitar Solo

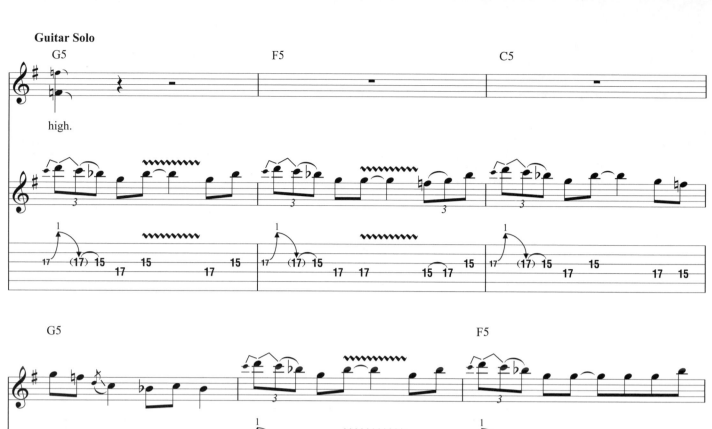

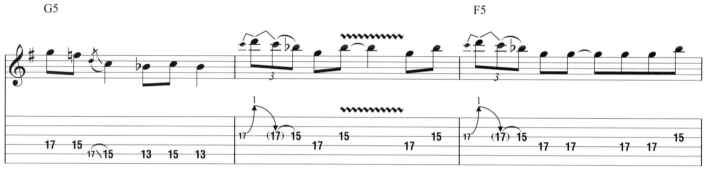

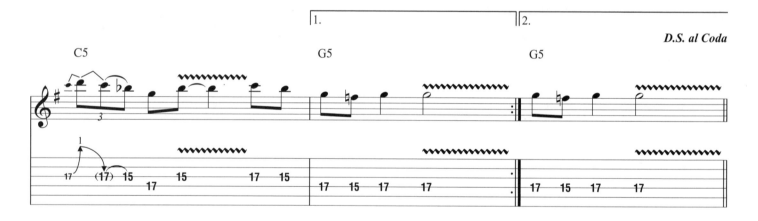

D.S. al Coda

$\oplus$ **Coda**

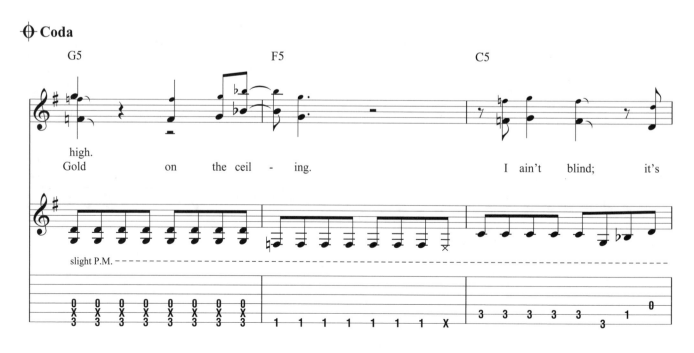

high.
Gold on the ceil - ing. I ain't blind; it's

slight P.M. -

just a mat - ter of time be - fore you steal ___ it.

slight P.M. -

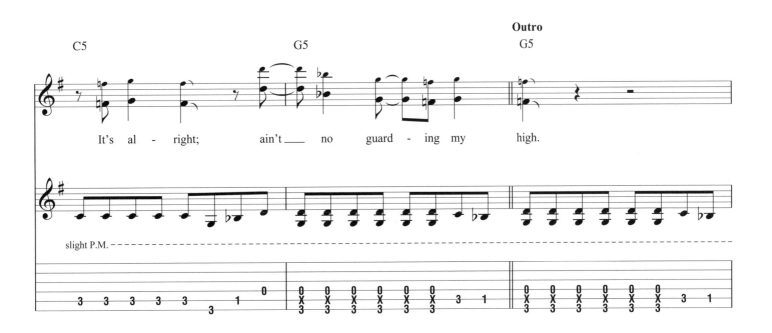

Outro

It's al - right; ain't ___ no guard - ing my high.

slight P.M. -

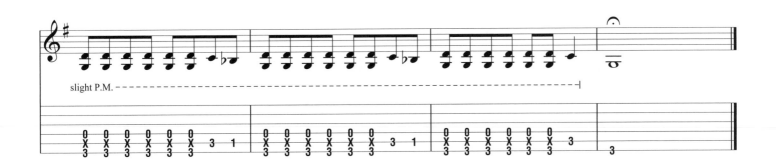

slight P.M. -

Additional Lyrics

2. Clouds covered love's barbed-wire stare.
   Strung up, strung out; I just can't go without.
   I could never drown in.

Heaven

Words and Music by Henry Garza, Joey Garza and Ringo Garza

Tune down 1/2 step:
(low to high) E♭-A♭-D♭-G♭-B♭-E♭

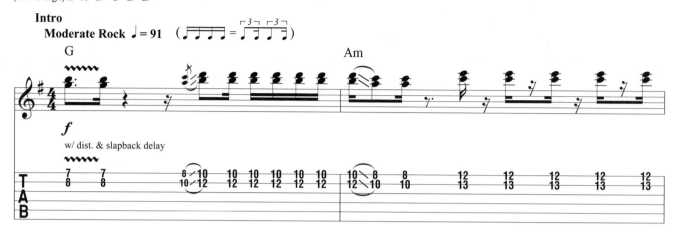

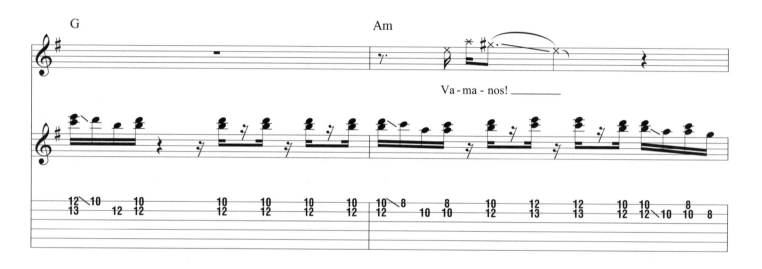

Va - ma - nos!

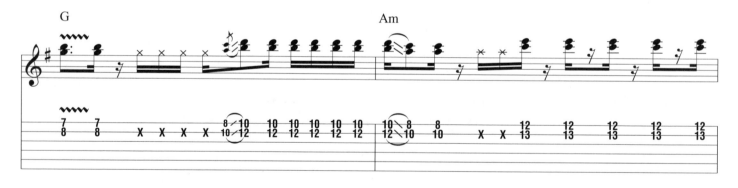

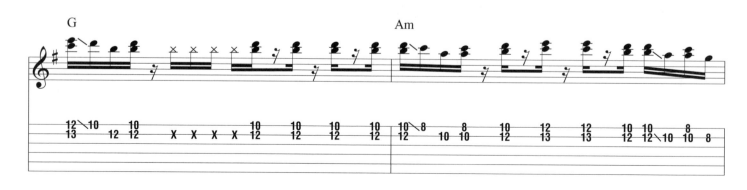

Copyright © 2004 EMI Blackwood Music Inc.
All Rights Administered by Sony/ATV Music Publishing LLC, 424 Church Street, Suite 1200, Nashville, TN 37219
International Copyright Secured   All Rights Reserved

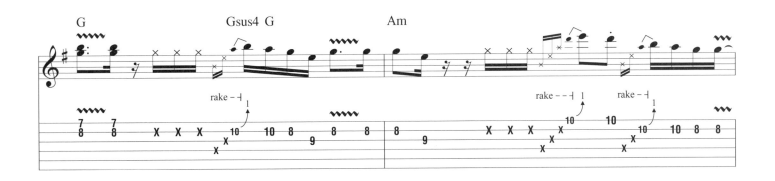

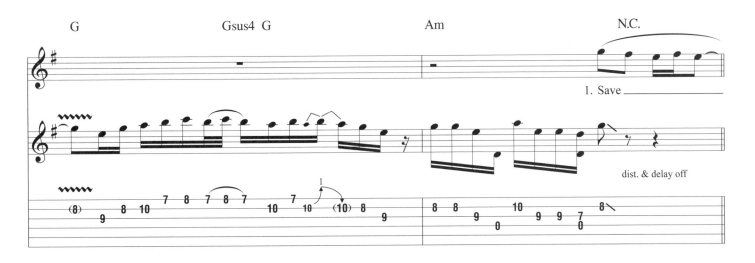

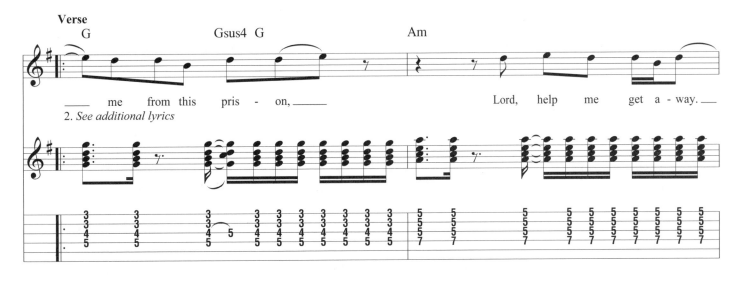

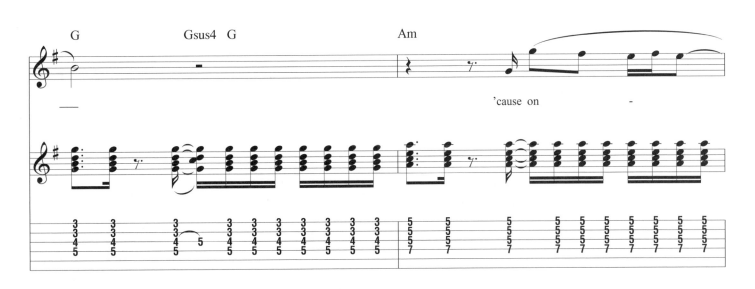

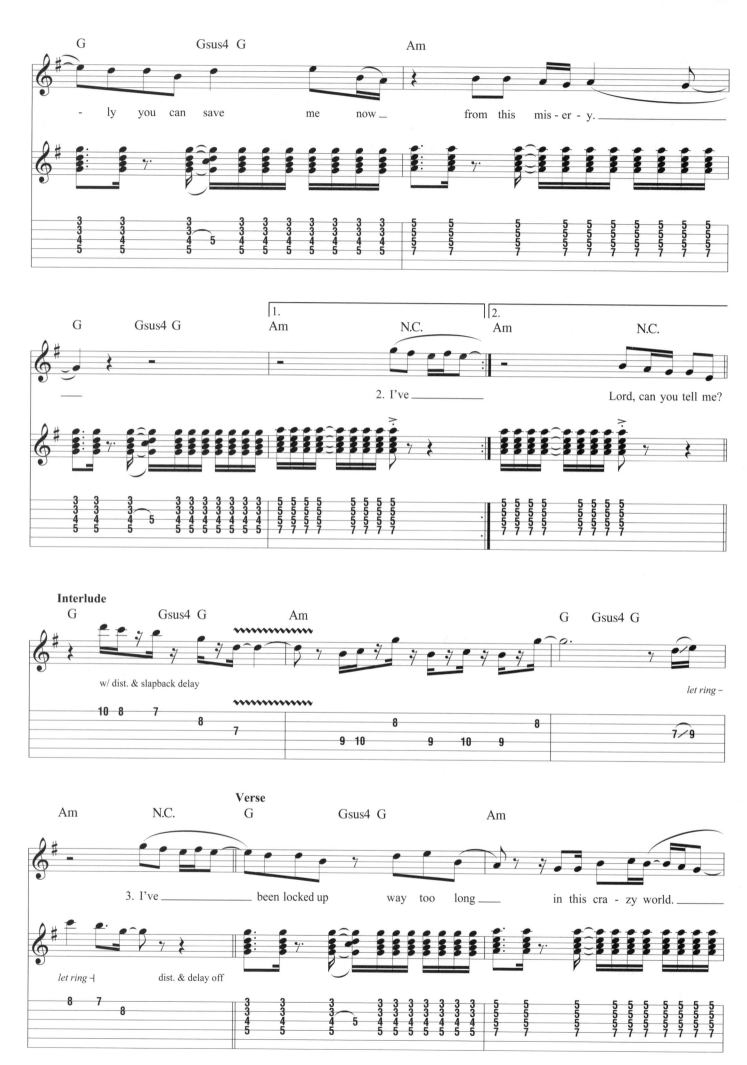

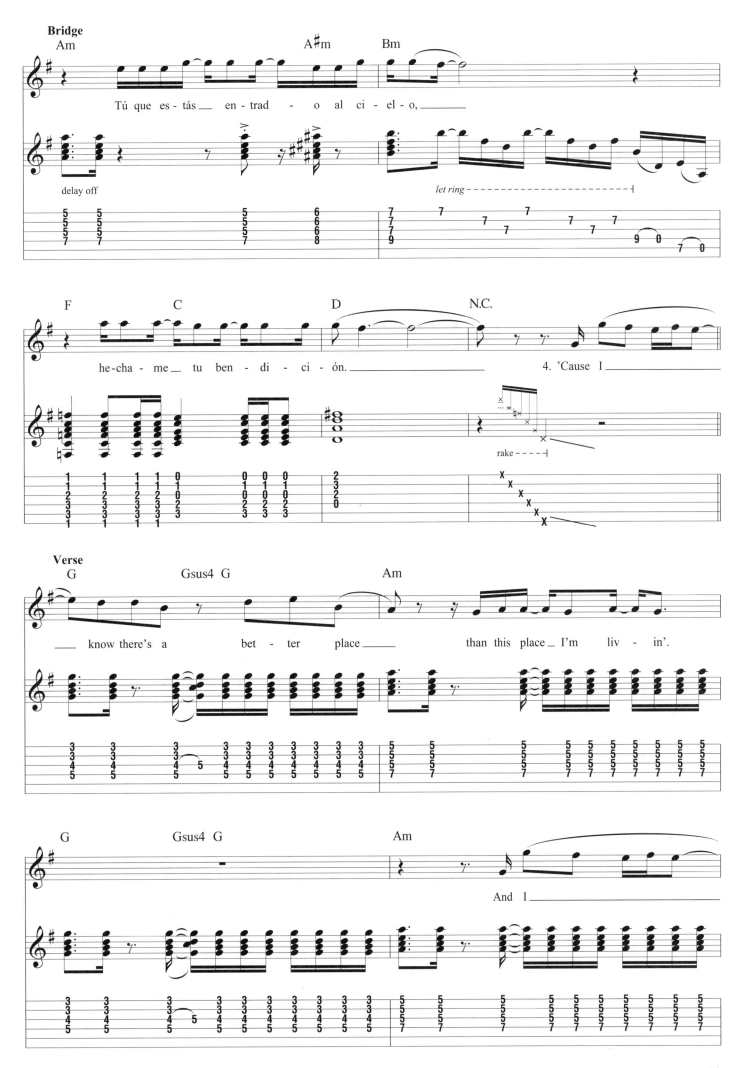

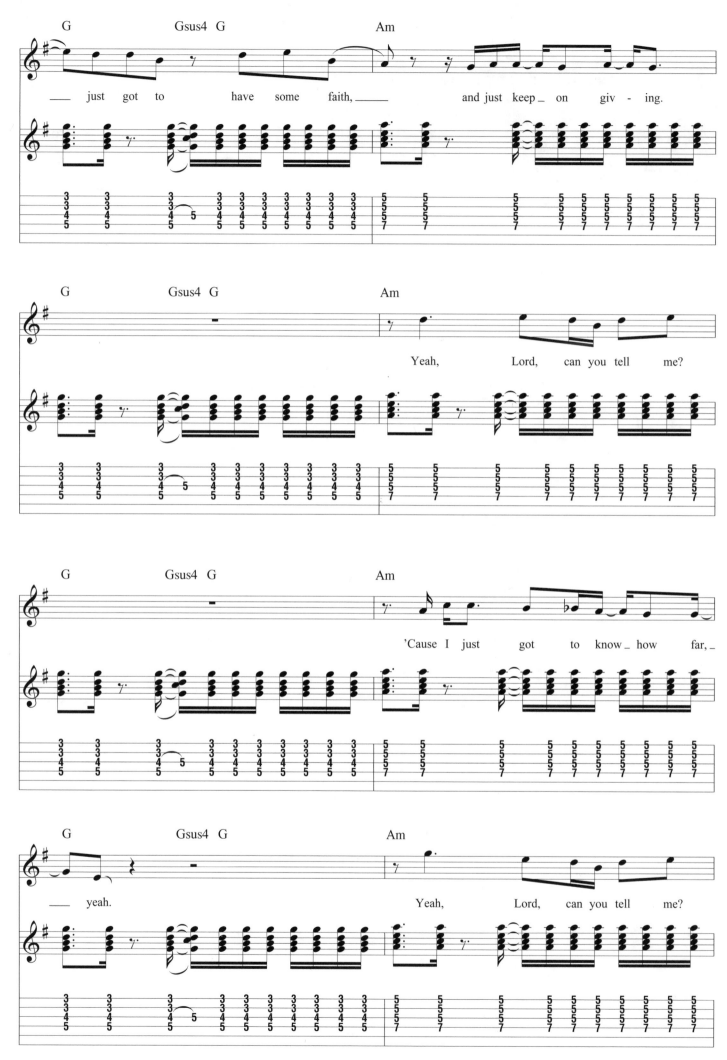

Outro-Guitar Solo

'Cause I just got-ta know＿ how far.＿

I just wan-na know＿ how far.＿

w/ dist. & slapback delay

let ring

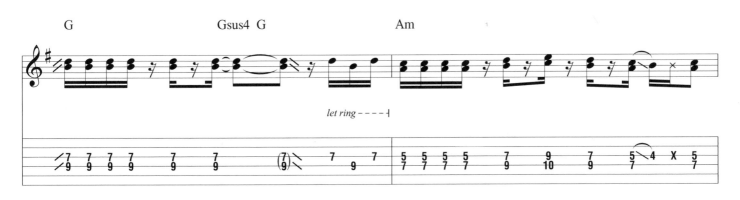

let ring

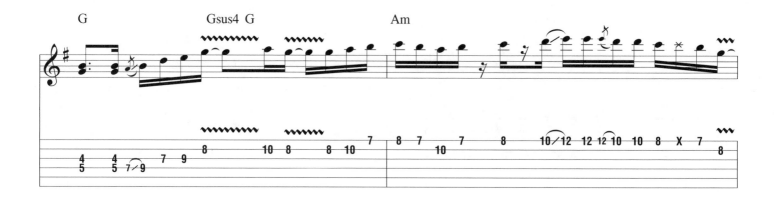

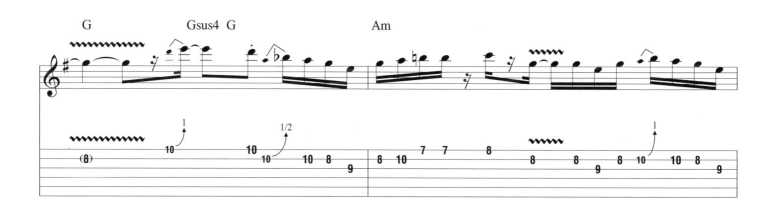

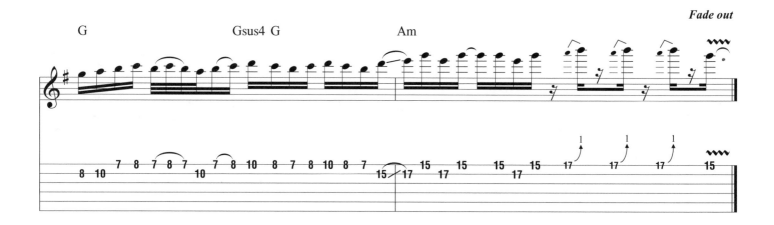

Additional Lyrics

2. I've been lost in my own place
   And I'm gettin' weary.
   And I know that I need to change
   My ways of livin'.
   Lord, can you tell me?

How You Remind Me

Words by Chad Kroeger
Music by Nickelback

Drop D tuning:
(low to high) D-A-D-G-B-E

Verse
Moderately slow ♩ = 86

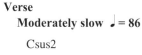

1. Nev-er made it as a wise man. I could-n't cut it as a poor man steal-in'.

Tired of liv-in' like a blind man. I'm sick of sight with-out a sense of feel-in'.

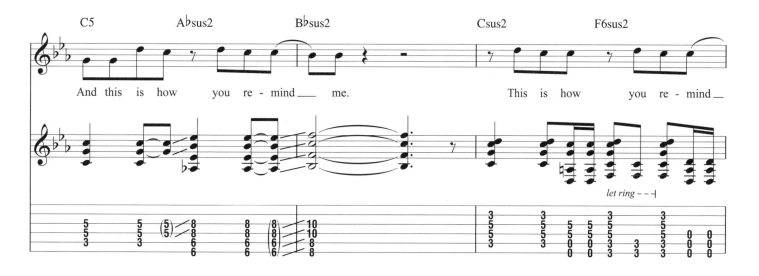

And this is how you re-mind___ me. This is how you re-mind___

© 2001 WARNER-TAMERLANE PUBLISHING CORP., ARM YOUR DILLO PUBLISHING INC.,
BLACK DIESEL MUSIC, INC., ZERO G MUSIC INC. and LADEKIV MUSIC INC.
All Rights Administered by WARNER-TAMERLANE PUBLISHING CORP.
All Rights Reserved   Used by Permission

Kryptonite

Words and Music by Matt Roberts, Brad Arnold and Todd Harrell

Copyright © 2000 SONGS OF UNIVERSAL, INC. and ESCATAWPA SONGS
All Rights Controlled and Administered by SONGS OF UNIVERSAL, INC.
All Rights Reserved   Used by Permission

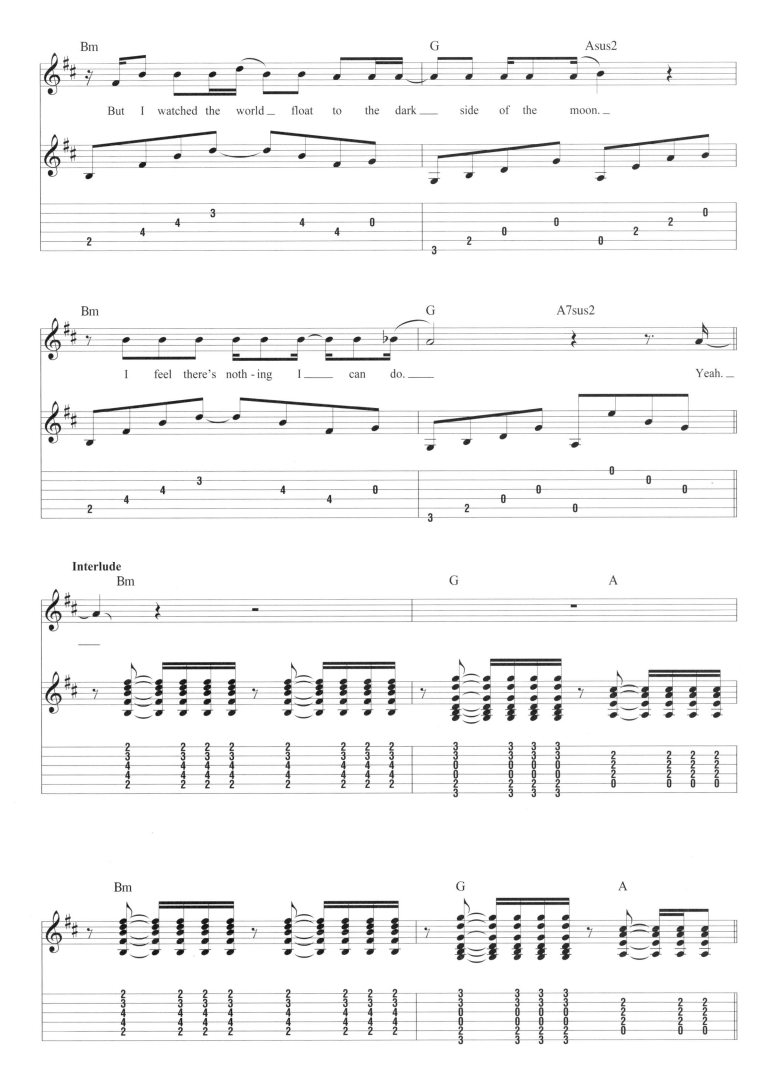

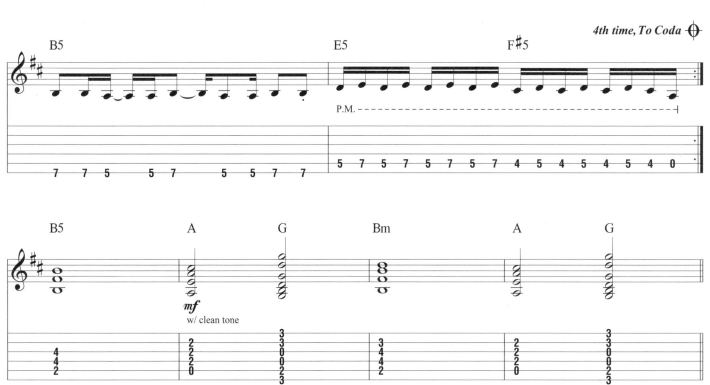

Additional Lyrics

3. You called me strong, you called me weak,
But still your secrets I will keep.
You took for granted all the times I never let you down.
You stumbled in and bumped your head.
If not for me, then you'd be dead.
I picked you up and put you back on solid ground.

No One Knows

Words and Music by Mark Lanegan, Josh Homme and Nick Oliveri

Tune down 2 steps:
(low to high) C-F-B♭-E♭-G-C

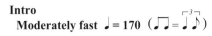

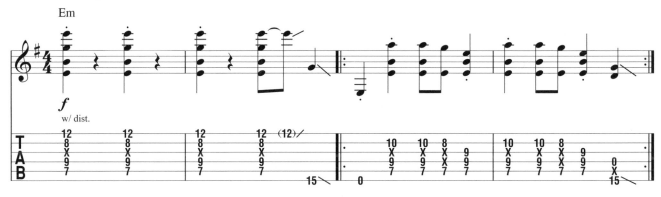

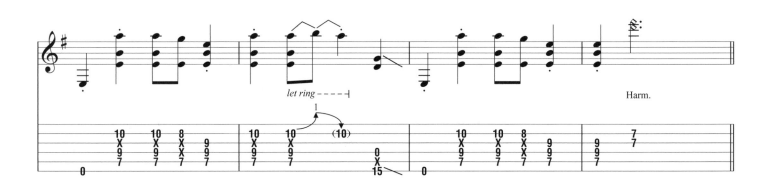

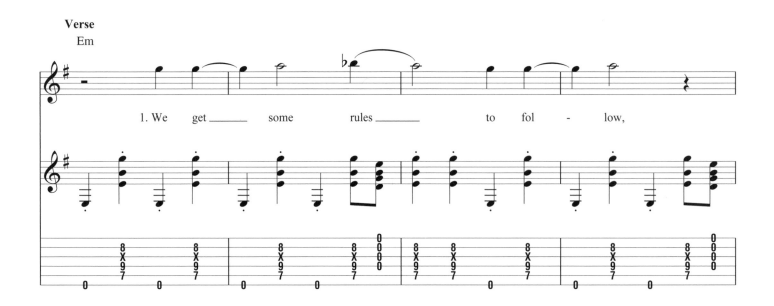

Copyright © 2002 Heavenly Songs, Ripplestick Music, Board Stiff Music and Natural Light Music
All Rights on behalf of Heavenly Songs and Ripplestick Music Administered by
Sony/ATV Music Publishing LLC, 424 Church Street, Suite 1200, Nashville, TN 37219
All Rights on behalf of Board Stiff Music Administered Worldwide by Songs Of Kobalt Music Publishing
International Copyright Secured   All Rights Reserved

And I

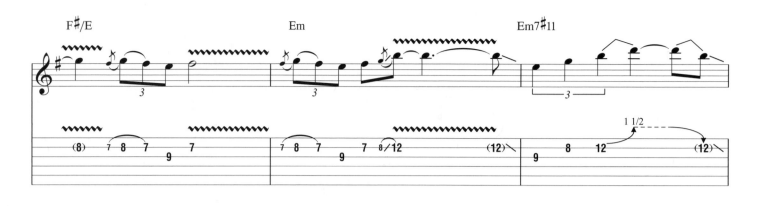

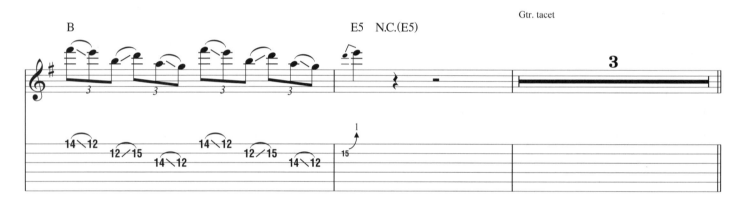

Verse

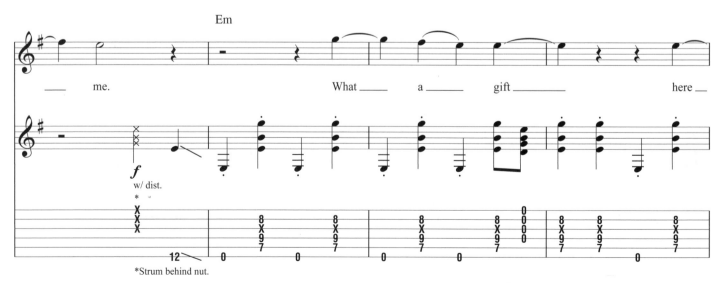

Plush

Words and Music by Scott Weiland, Dean DeLeo, Robert DeLeo and Eric Kretz

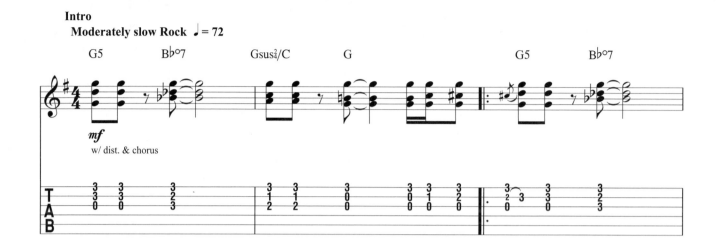

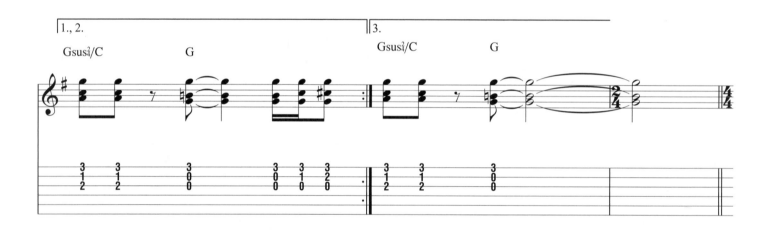

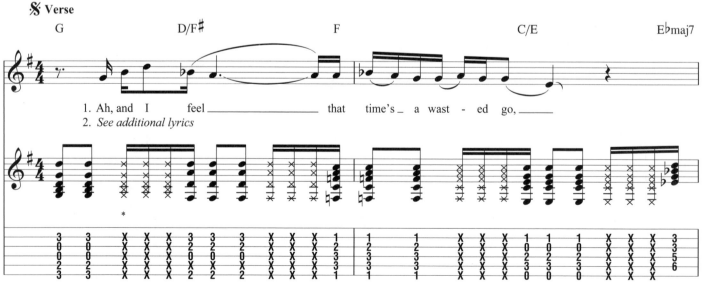

*Muted strings produce occasional random harmonics throughout.

Copyright © 1992 MILKSONGS and TRIPLE KAUF NOPLATE MUZAK
All Rights Controlled and Administered by UNIVERSAL MUSIC CORP.
All Rights Reserved   Used by Permission

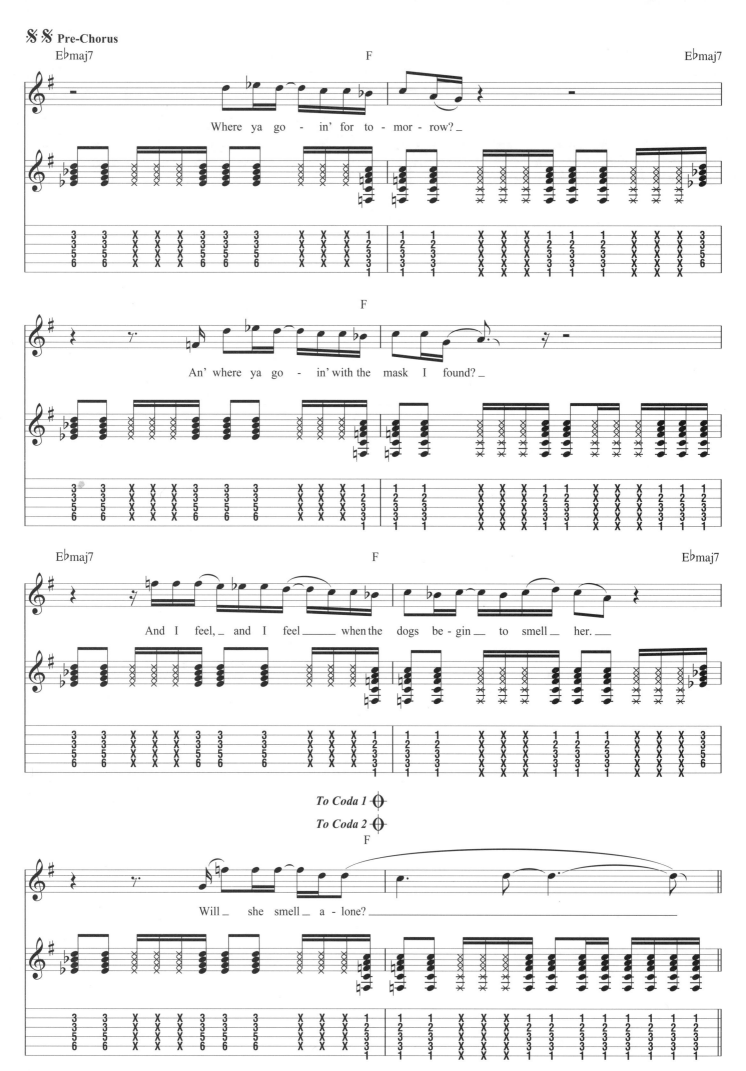

Outro

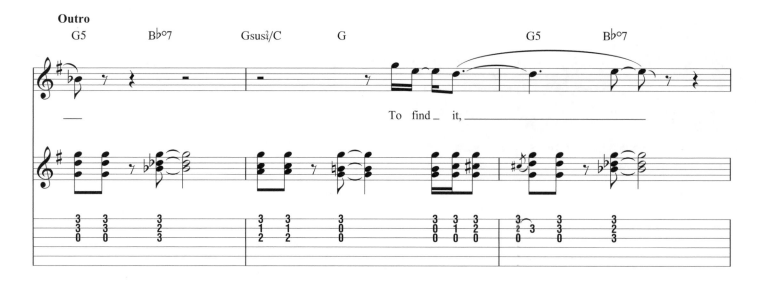

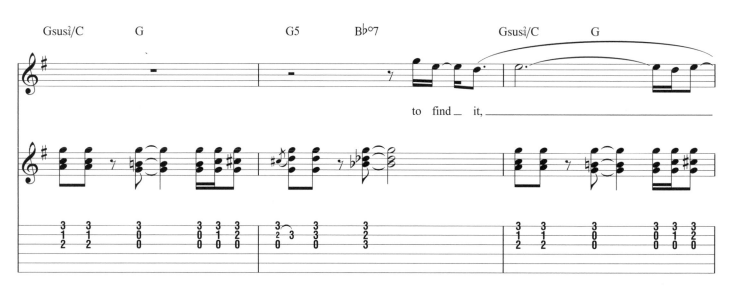

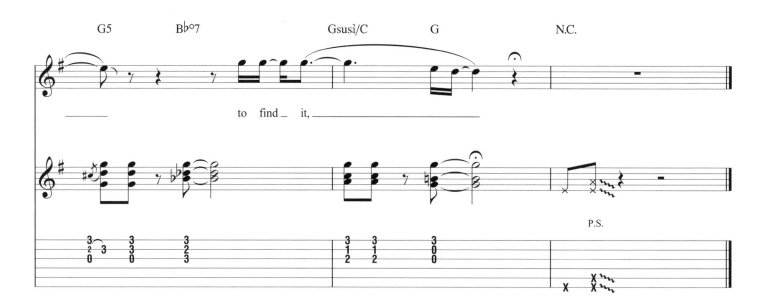

Additional Lyrics

2. Ah, and I feel so much depends on the weather,
    So is it raining in your bedroom?
    And I see that these are the eyes of disarray.
    So would you even care?

The Pretender

Words and Music by Dave Grohl, Taylor Hawkins, Christopher Shiflett and Nate Mendel

Copyright © 2007 SONGS OF UNIVERSAL, INC., LIVING UNDER A ROCK MUSIC, MJ Twelve MUSIC,
I LOVE THE PUNK ROCK MUSIC and FLYING EARFORM MUSIC
All Rights for MJ TWELVE MUSIC and I LOVE THE PUNK ROCK MUSIC Controlled and Administered by SONGS OF UNIVERSAL, INC.
All Rights for LIVING UNDER A ROCK MUSIC Controlled and Administered by UNIVERSAL MUSIC CORP.
All Rights for FLYING EARFORM MUSIC Administered by BMG RIGHTS MANAGEMENT (US) LLC
All Rights Reserved   Used by Permission

To Coda 1

To Coda 2

you re-fuse __ to hear. __   I'm __ the face __ that you have __ to face, __

slight P.M. ------------⌐   slight P.M. ----⌐   slight P.M. ------------⌐   slight P.M. ----⌐

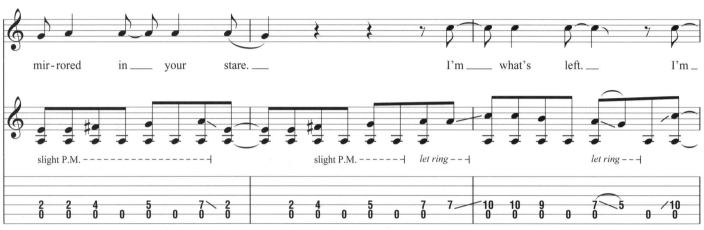

mir-rored in __ your stare. __   I'm __ what's left. __ I'm __

slight P.M. --------------------⌐   slight P.M. ------⌐   let ring --⌐   let ring --⌐

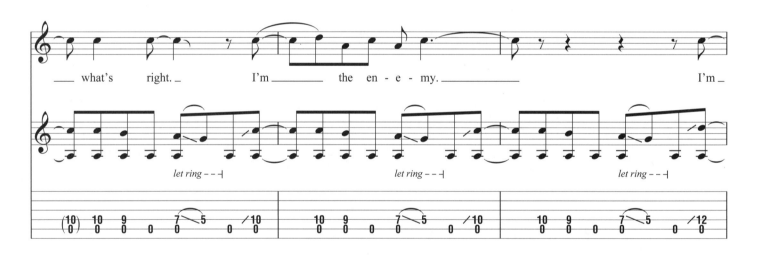

__ what's right. __ I'm __ the en-e-my. __   I'm __

let ring --⌐   let ring --⌐   let ring --⌐

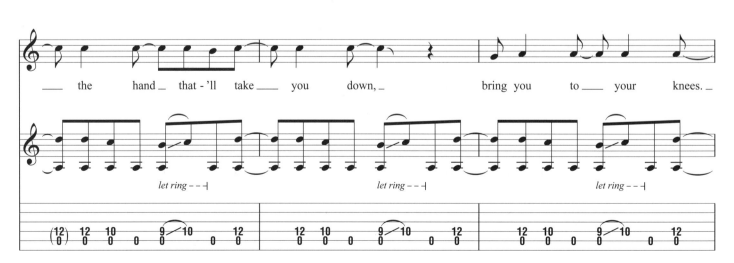

__ the hand __ that-'ll take __ you down, __ bring you to __ your knees. __

let ring --⌐   let ring --⌐   let ring --⌐

Seven Nation Army

Words and Music by Jack White

Open A tuning:
(low to high) E-A-E-A-C#-E

Intro
Moderate Rock ♩ = 122

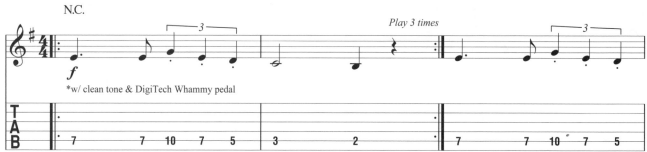

*w/ clean tone & DigiTech Whammy pedal

*Whammy pedal set for 1 octave down and kept in toe-down position throughout. Sounds 1 octave lower than written while pedal is engaged.

𝄋 Verse
2nd & 3rd times, substitute Fill 1 (7 1/2 times)

1. I'm gon-na fight 'em off, ___ a sev-en na-tion
2., 3. See additional lyrics

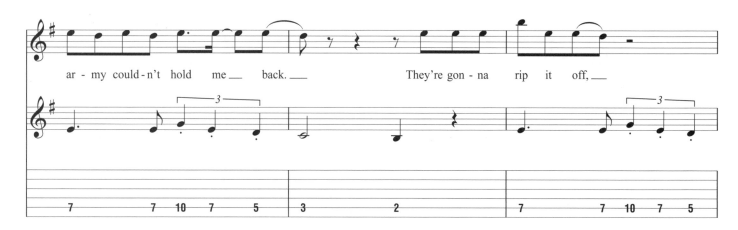

ar-my could-n't hold me ___ back. ___ They're gon-na rip it off, ___

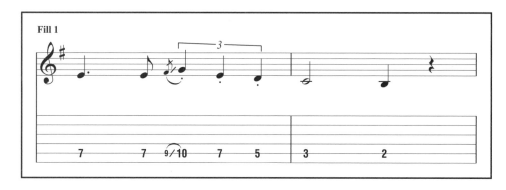

Fill 1

Copyright © 2003 PEPPERMINT STRIPE MUSIC
All Rights Administered by SONGS OF UNIVERSAL, INC.
All Rights Reserved   Used by Permission

taking their time right behind my back. And I'm

talking to myself at night because I can't forget.

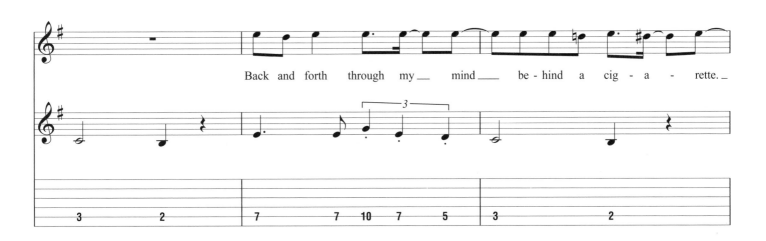

Back and forth through my mind behind a cigarette.

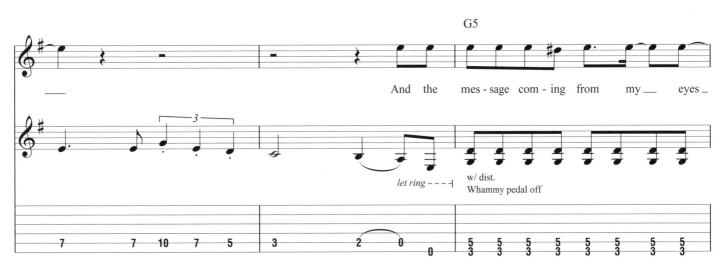

And the message coming from my eyes

2. Don't wan - na

Coda 1

Guitar Solo

D.S. al Coda 2

Coda 2

Outro

Additional Lyrics

2. Don't wanna hear about it, ev'ry single one's got a story to tell.
Ev'ryone knows about it, from the Queen of England to the hounds of hell.
And if I catch it coming back my way, I'm gonna serve it to you.
And that ain't what you want to hear, but that's what I'll do.
And the feeling coming from my bones says find a home.

3. I'm goin' to Wichita, far from this opera forevermore.
I'm gonna work the straw, make the sweat drip out of every pore.
And I'm bleeding, and I'm bleeding, and I'm bleeding right before the Lord.
All the words are gonna bleed from me and I will think no more.
And the stains coming from my blood tell me go back home.

Smooth

Words by Rob Thomas
Music by Rob Thomas and Itaal Shur

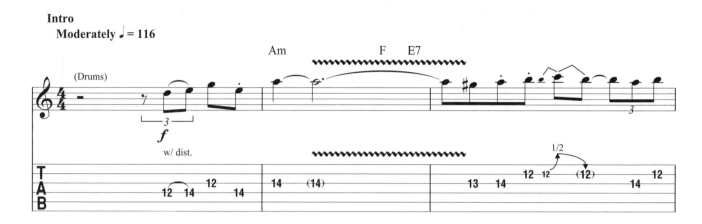

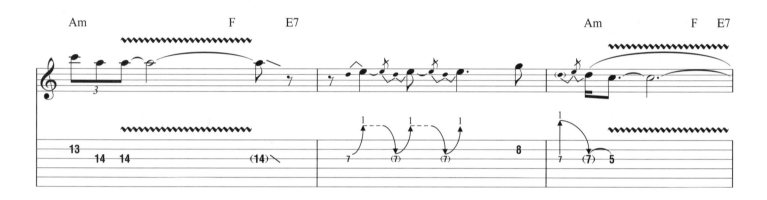

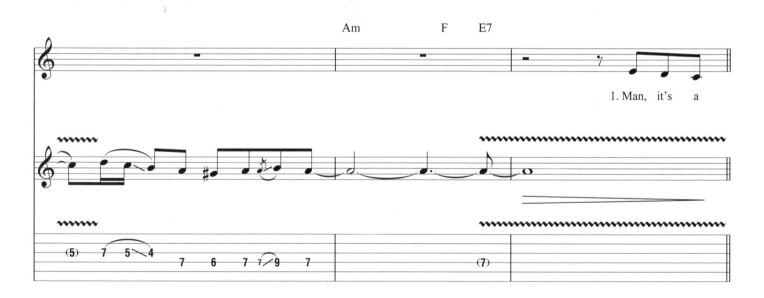

Copyright © 1999 EMI April Music Inc., EMI Blackwood Music Inc., U Rule Music, Warner-Tamerlane Publishing Corp. and Itaal Shur Music
All Rights on behalf of EMI April Music Inc., EMI Blackwood Music Inc. and U Rule Music Administered by
Sony/ATV Music Publishing LLC, 424 Church Street, Suite 1200, Nashville, TN 37219
All Rights on behalf of Itaal Shur Music Administered by Downtown DMP Songs
International Copyright Secured   All Rights Reserved

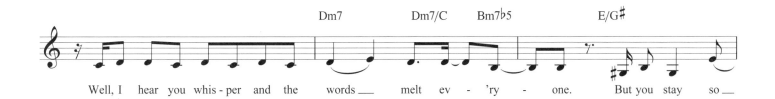

Well, I hear you whis-per and the words ___ melt ev-'ry - one. But you stay so ___

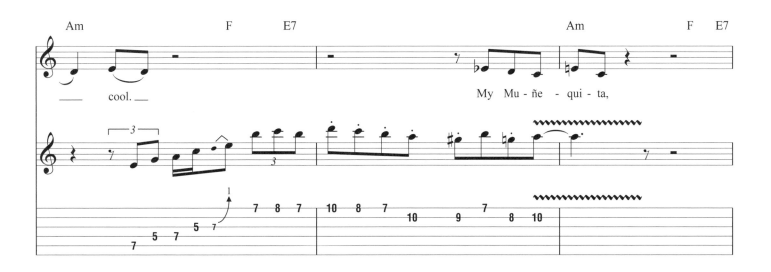

___ cool. ___

My Mu - ñe - qui - ta,

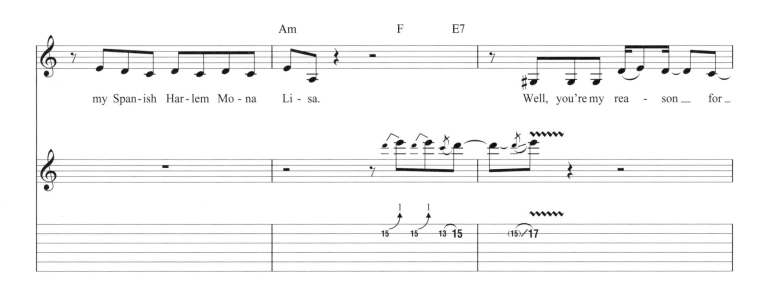

my Span-ish Har-lem Mo - na Li - sa.

Well, you're my rea - son ___ for ___

___ rea - son, ___

the ___ step in my groove, ___

yeah. ___

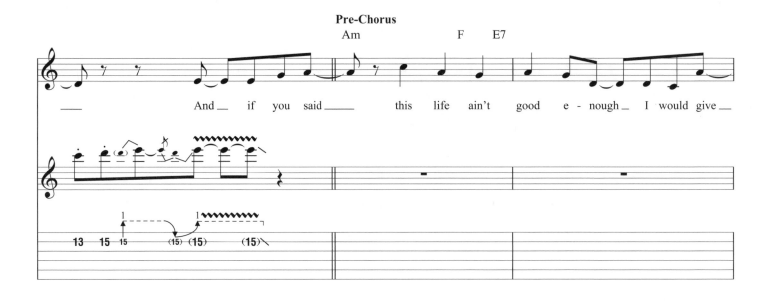

Pre-Chorus

And — if you said — this life ain't good e - nough — I would give —

Gtr. tacet

— my world to lift you up. — I could change — my life to

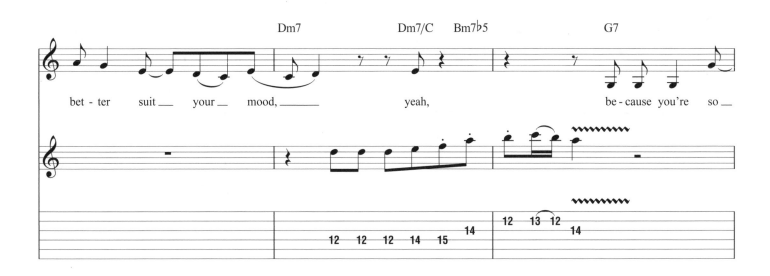

bet - ter suit — your — mood, — yeah, be - cause you're so —

Chorus

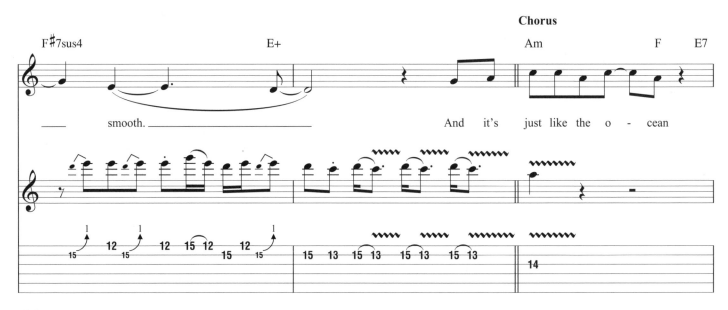

— smooth. And it's just like the o - cean

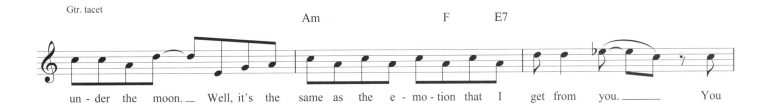

Gtr. tacet

Am   F   E7

un - der the moon. __ Well, it's the same as the e - mo - tion that I get from you. _____ You

Am   F   E7   Dm   E+

got the kind of lov - in' that can be so smooth, __ yeah.   Gim - me your heart, __ make it real __

Interlude

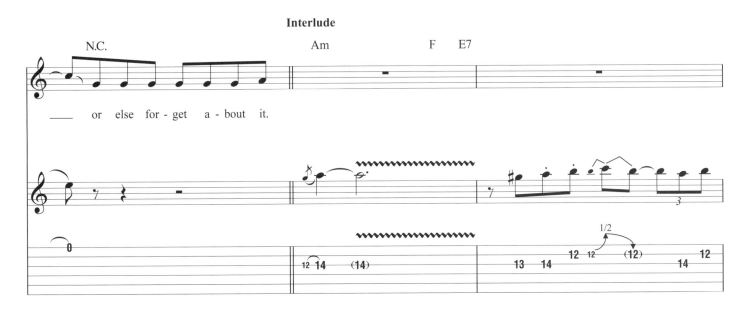

N.C.   Am   F   E7

___ or else for - get a - bout it.

Verse

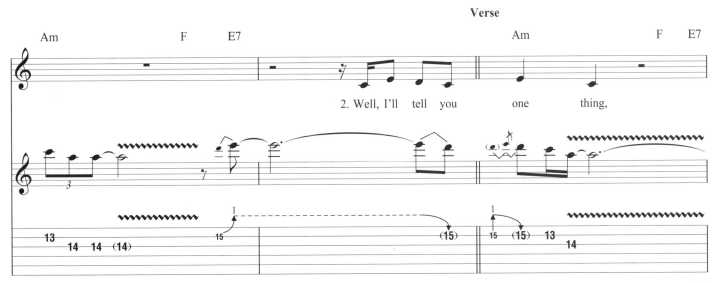

Am   F   E7   Am   F   E7

2. Well, I'll tell you one thing,

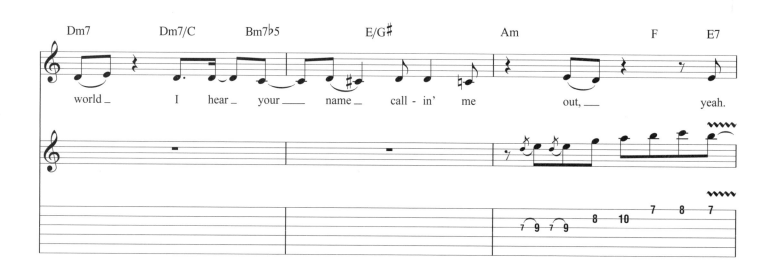

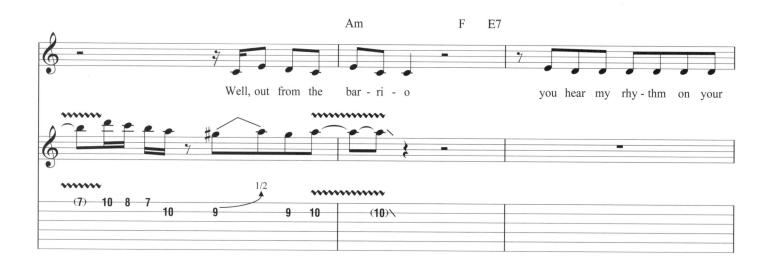

Pre-Chorus

Gtr. tacet

slow, __ turn - in' __ you __ 'round __ and __ 'round. And if you said __ this life ain't good e - nough, __ I would give __ my world to lift you up. __ I could change __ my life to bet - ter suit __ your __ mood. __ Yeah. Be - cause you're so __ smooth. __

Chorus

Well, and it's just like the o - cean un - der the moon. __ Well, it's the

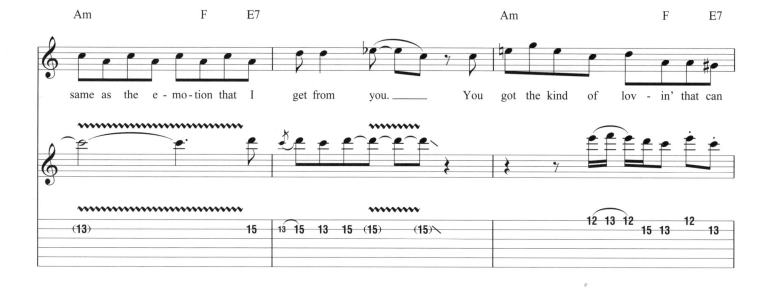

same as the e-mo-tion that I get from you.____ You got the kind of lov- in' that can

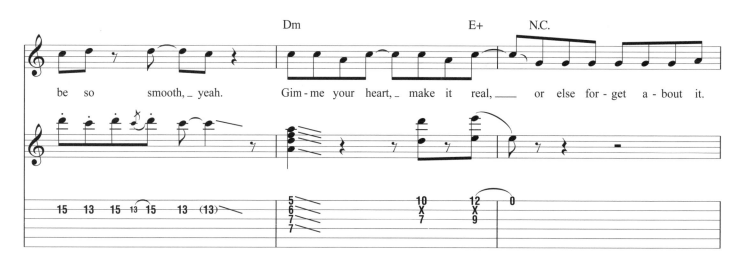

be so smooth, _ yeah. Gim-me your heart, _ make it real, ____ or else for-get a-bout it.

Guitar Solo

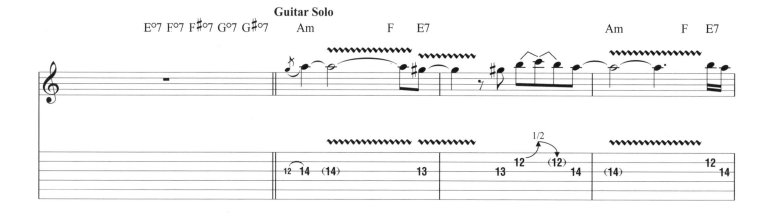

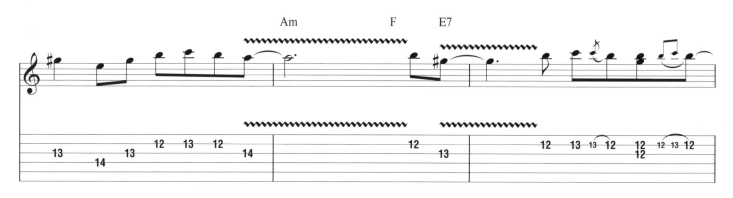

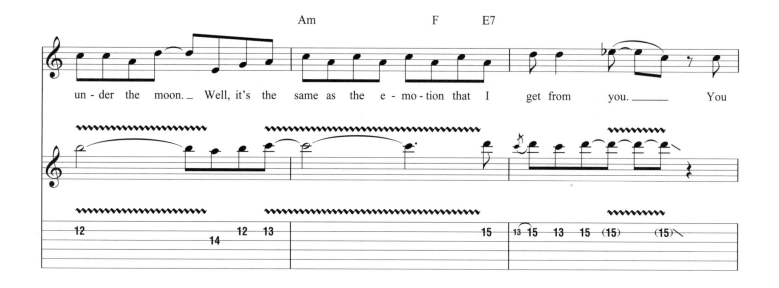

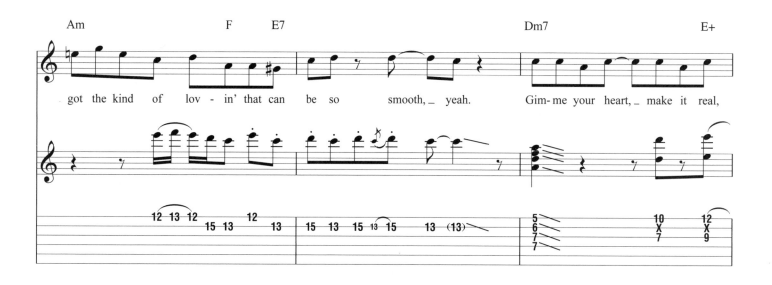

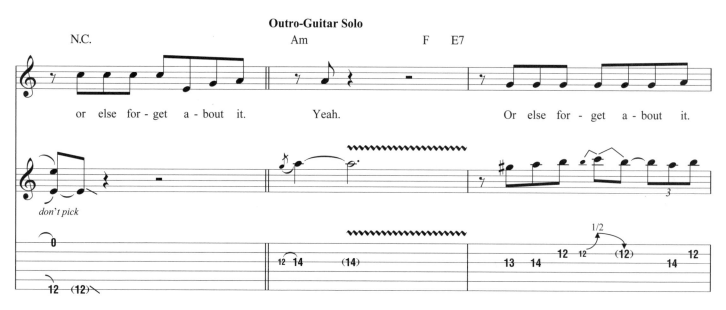

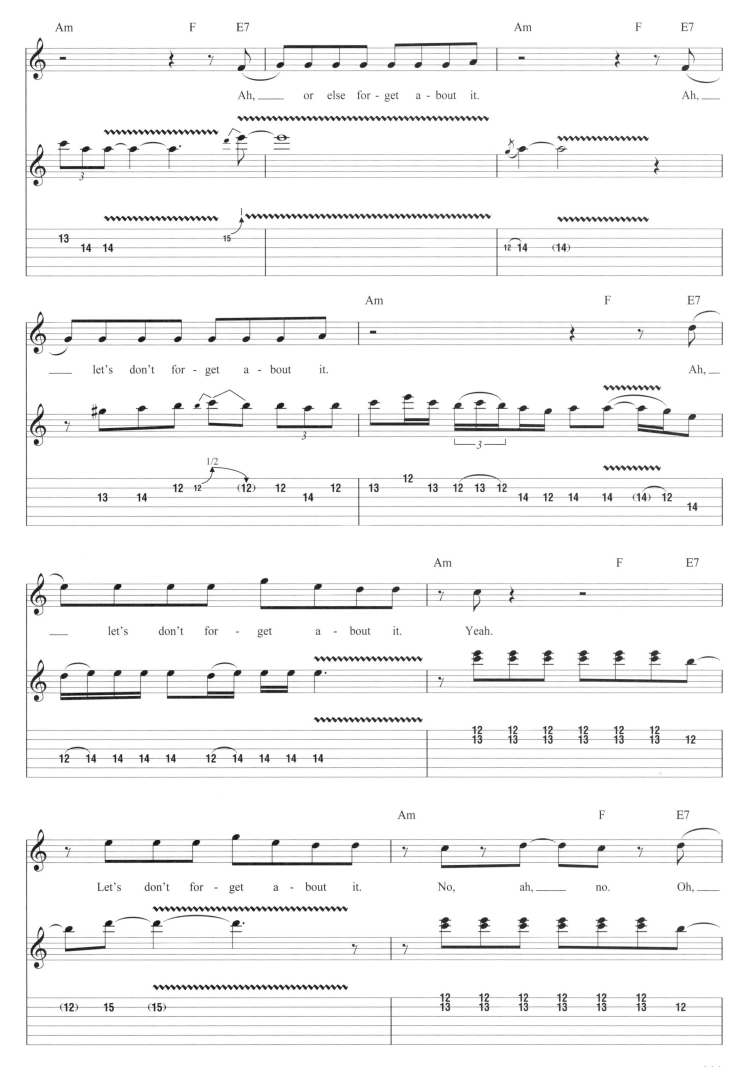

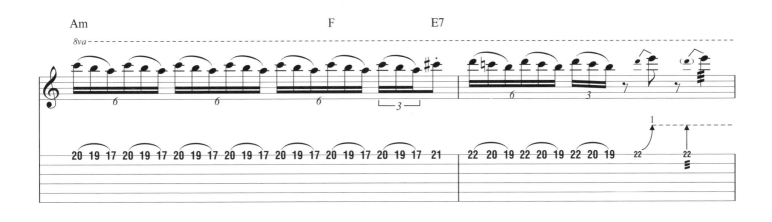

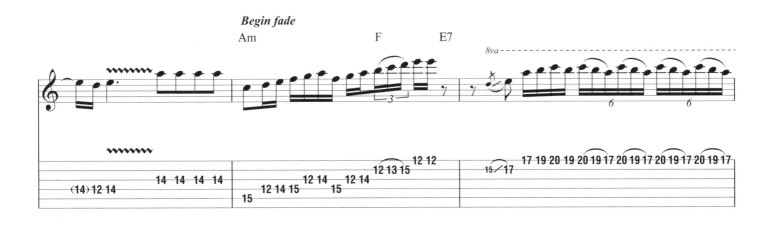

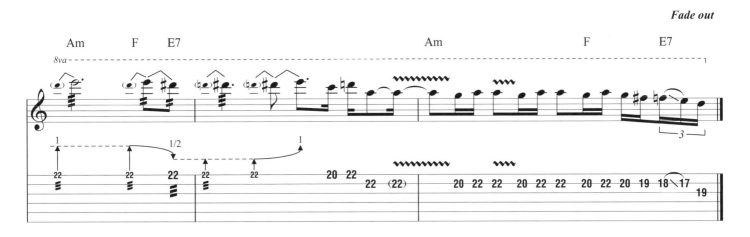

Under the Bridge

Words and Music by Anthony Kiedis, Flea, John Frusciante and Chad Smith

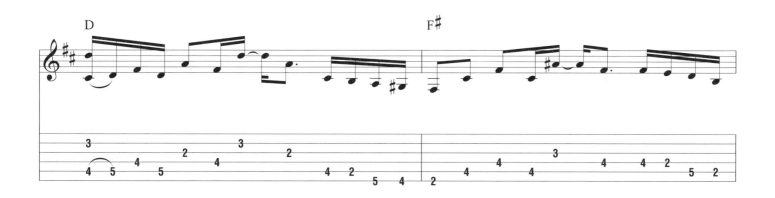

© 1991 MOEBETOBLAME MUSIC
All Rights Reserved   Used by Permission

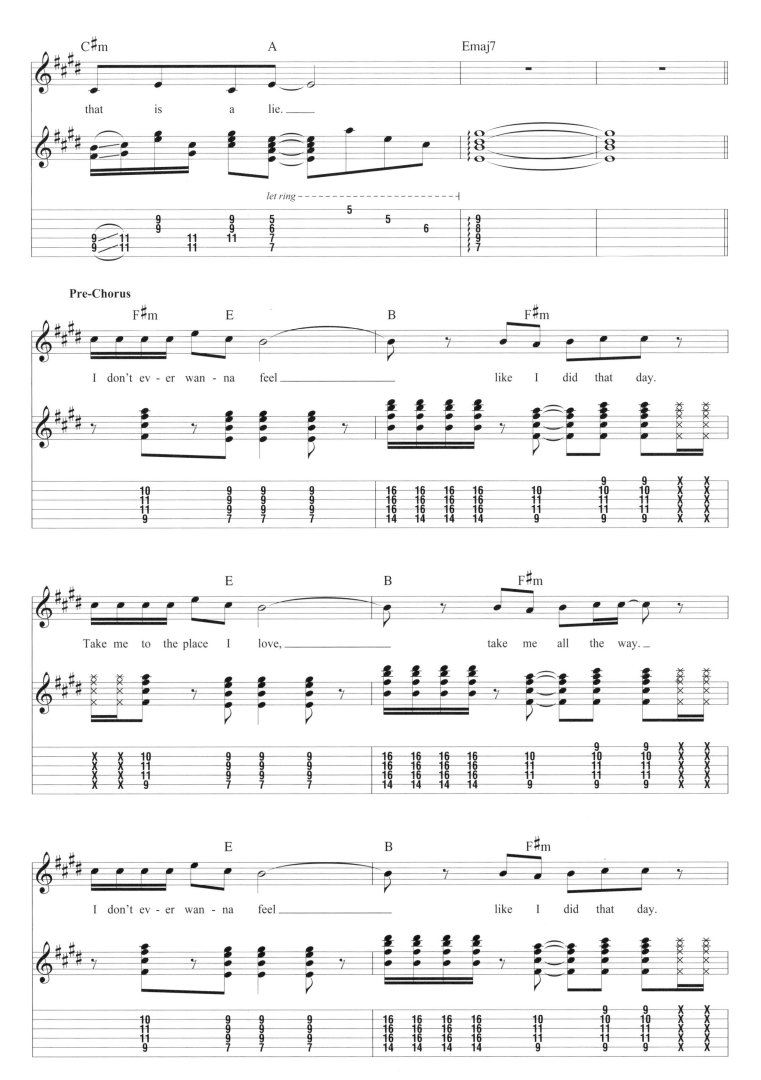

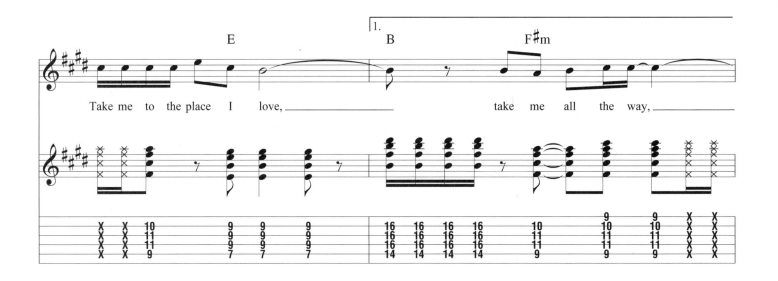

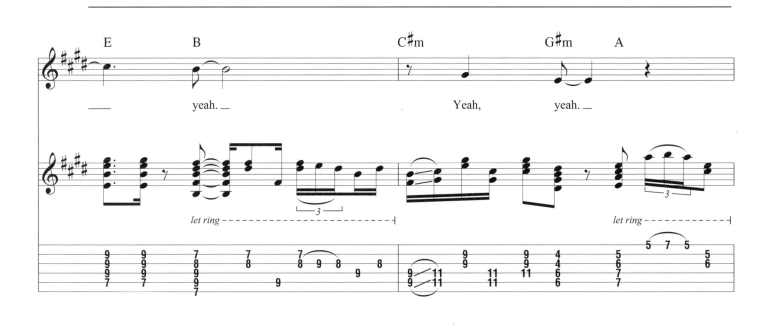

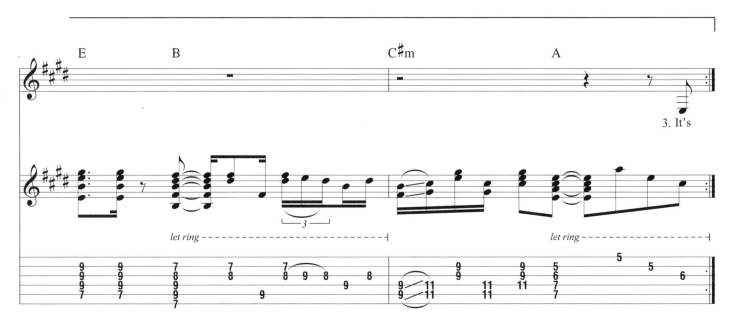

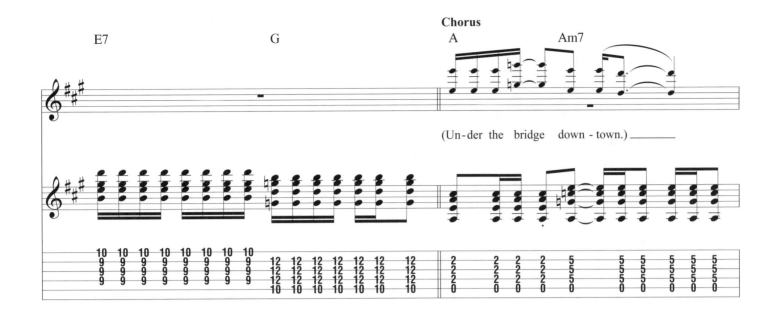

(Un-der the bridge down - town.) _____

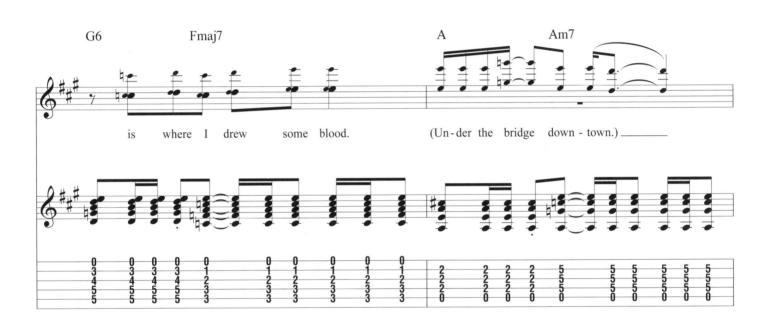

is where I drew some blood. (Un-der the bridge down - town.) _____

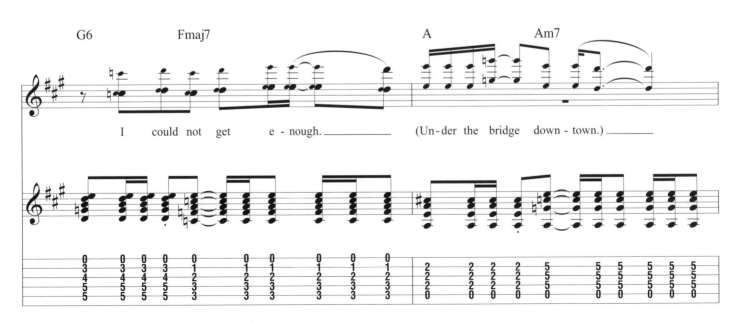

I could not get e - nough. _____ (Un-der the bridge down - town.) _____

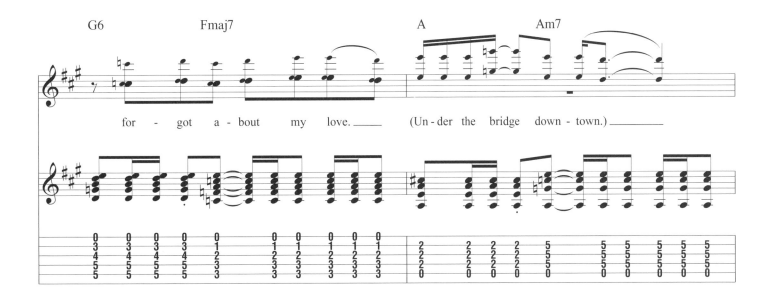

for - got a - bout my love. _____ (Un - der the bridge down - town.) _____

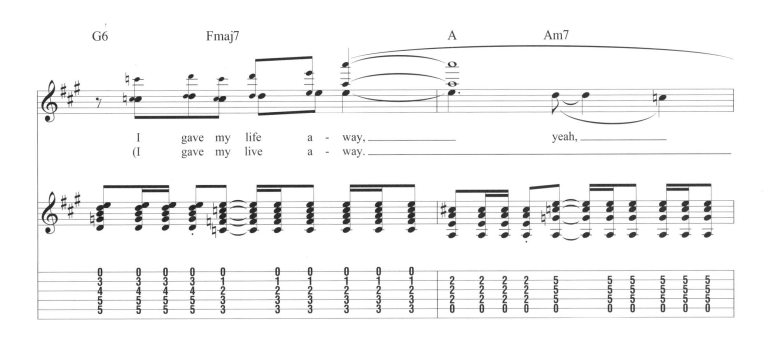

I gave my life a - way, _____ yeah, _____
(I gave my live a - way. _____

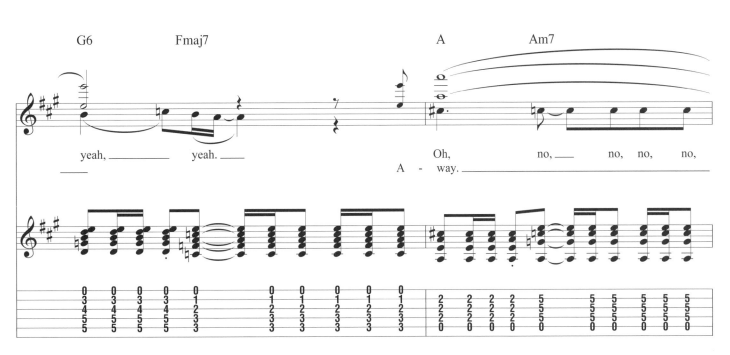

yeah, _____ yeah. _____ Oh, no, _____ no, no, no,
_____ A - way. _____

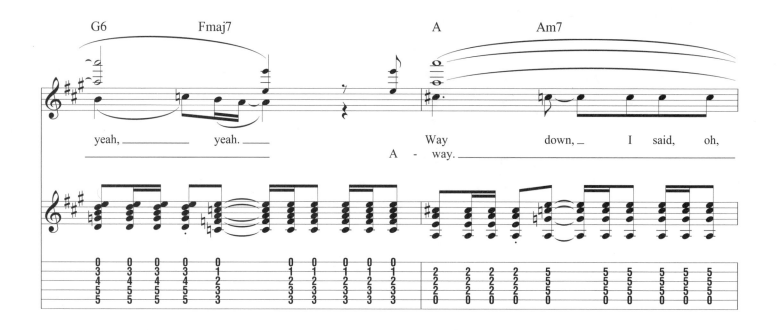

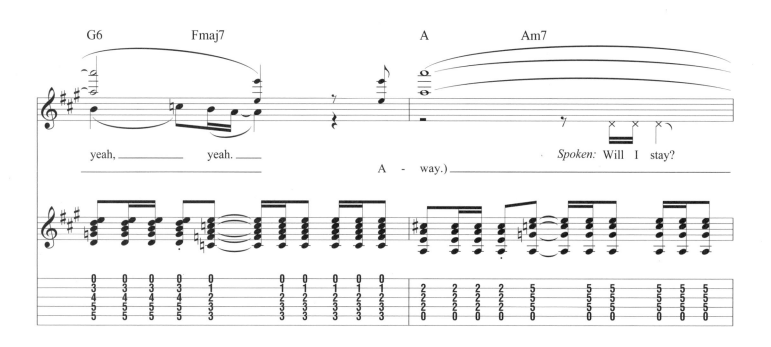

Outro

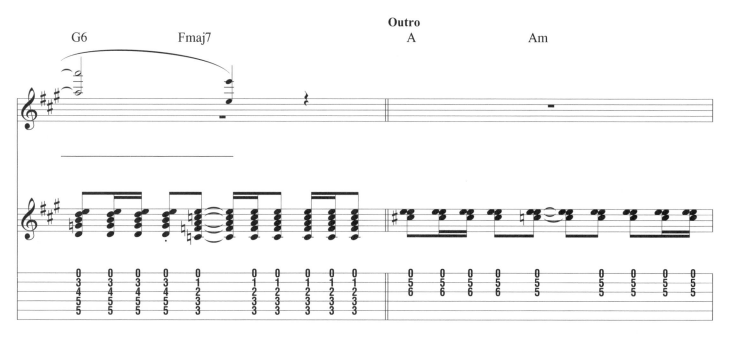

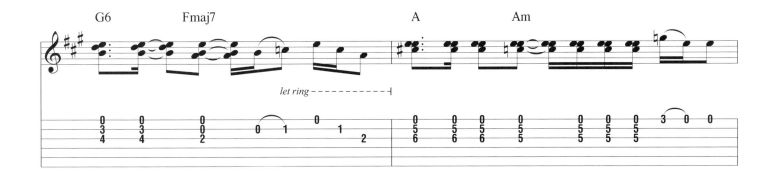

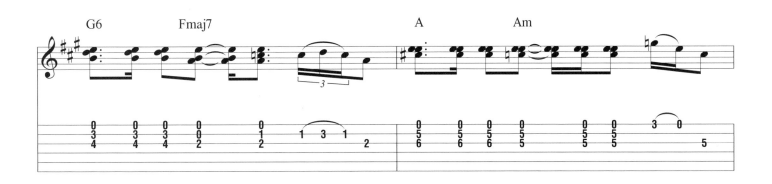

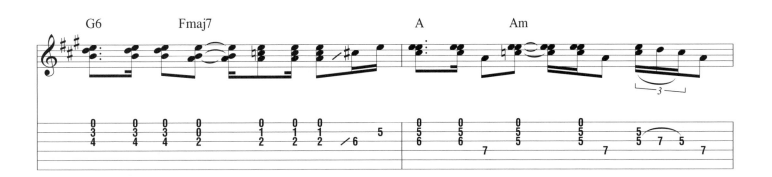

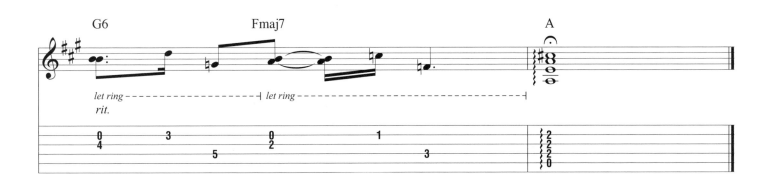

Additional Lyrics

3. It's hard to believe that there's nobody out there.
   It's hard to believe that I'm all alone.
   At least I have her love, the city, she loves me.
   Lonely as I am, together we cry.

Yellow Ledbetter

Lyrics as felt by Eddie Vedder
Music by Jeff Ament and Mike McCready

Copyright © 1991 INNOCENT BYSTANDER, SCRIBING C-MENT SONGS, JUMPIN' CAT MUSIC and UNIVERSAL MUSIC WORKS
All Rights administered by UNIVERSAL MUSIC WORKS
All Rights Reserved. Used by Permission.

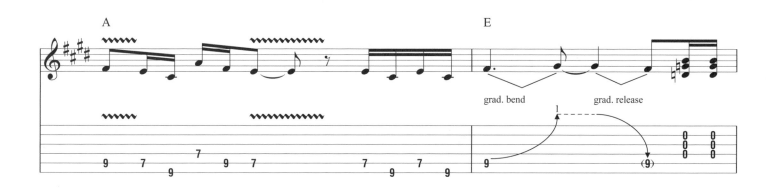

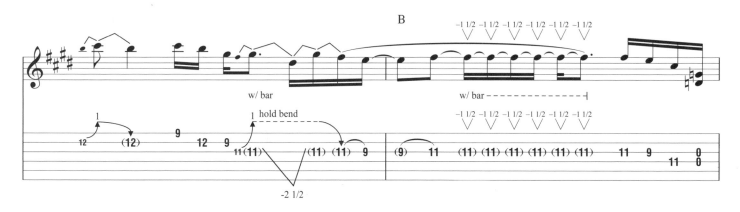

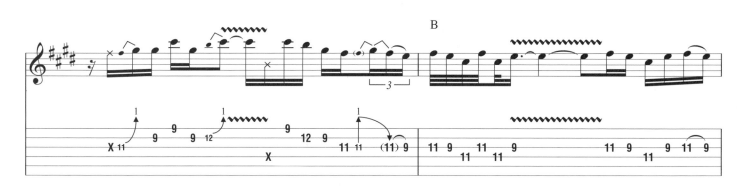

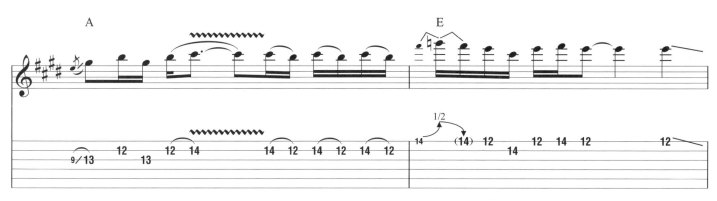

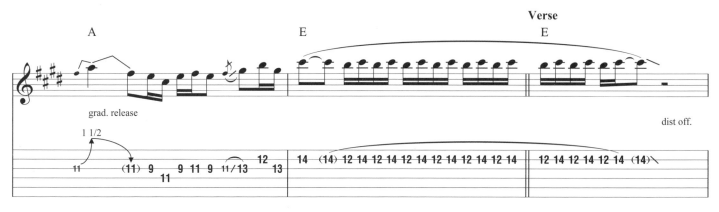

Outro

DELUXE GUITAR PLAY-ALONG

AUDIO ACCESS INCLUDED 🔊

The Deluxe Guitar Play-Along series will help you play songs faster than ever before! Accurate, easy-to-read guitar tab and professional, customizable audio for 15 songs. The interactive, online audio interface includes tempo/pitch control, looping, buttons to turn instruments on or off, and guitar tab with follow-along marker. The price of each book includes access to audio tracks online using the unique code inside. The tracks can also be downloaded and played offline. Now including PLAYBACK+, a multi-functional audio player that allows you to slow down audio, change pitch, set loop points, and pan left or right – available exclusively from Hal Leonard.

1. TOP ROCK HITS
Basket Case • Black Hole Sun • Come As You Are • Do I Wanna Know? • Gold on the Ceiling • Heaven • How You Remind Me • Kryptonite • No One Knows • Plush • The Pretender • Seven Nation Army • Smooth • Under the Bridge • Yellow Ledbetter.
00244758 Book/Online Audio $19.99

2. REALLY EASY SONGS
All the Small Things • Brain Stew • Californication • Free Fallin' • Helter Skelter • Hey Joe • Highway to Hell • Hurt (Quiet) • I Love Rock 'N Roll • Island in the Sun • Knockin' on Heaven's Door • La Bamba • Oh, Pretty Woman • Should I Stay or Should I Go • Smells Like Teen Spirit.
00244877 Book/Online Audio $19.99

3. ACOUSTIC SONGS
All Apologies • Banana Pancakes • Crash Into Me • Good Riddance (Time of Your Life) • Hallelujah • Hey There Delilah • Ho Hey • I Will Wait • I'm Yours • Iris • More Than Words • No Such Thing • Photograph • What I Got • Wonderwall.
00244709 Book/Online Audio $19.99

4. THE BEATLES
All My Loving • And I Love Her • Back in the U.S.S.R. • Don't Let Me Down • Get Back • A Hard Day's Night • Here Comes the Sun • I Will • In My Life • Let It Be • Michelle • Paperback Writer • Revolution • While My Guitar Gently Weeps • Yesterday.
00244968 Book/Online Audio $19.99

5. BLUES STANDARDS
Baby, What You Want Me to Do • Crosscut Saw • Double Trouble • Every Day I Have the Blues • Going Down • I'm Tore Down • I'm Your Hoochie Coochie Man • If You Love Me Like You Say • Just Your Fool • Killing Floor • Let Me Love You Baby • Messin' with the Kid • Pride and Joy • (They Call It) Stormy Monday (Stormy Monday Blues) • Sweet Home Chicago.
00245090 Book/Online Audio $19.99

6. RED HOT CHILI PEPPERS
The Adventures of Rain Dance Maggie • Breaking the Girl • Can't Stop • Dani California • Dark Necessities • Give It Away • My Friends • Otherside • Road Trippin' • Scar Tissue • Snow (Hey Oh) • Suck My Kiss • Tell Me Baby • Under the Bridge • The Zephyr Song.
00245089 Book/Online Audio $19.99

7. CLASSIC ROCK
Baba O'Riley • Born to Be Wild • Comfortably Numb • Dream On • Fortunate Son • Heartbreaker • Hotel California • Jet Airliner • More Than a Feeling • Old Time Rock & Roll • Rhiannon • Runnin' Down a Dream • Start Me Up • Sultans of Swing • Sweet Home Alabama.
00248381 Book/Online Audio $19.99

8. OZZY OSBOURNE
Bark at the Moon • Close My Eyes Forever • Crazy Train • Dreamer • Goodbye to Romance • I Don't Know • I Don't Wanna Stop • Mama, I'm Coming Home • Miracle Man • Mr. Crowley • No More Tears • Over the Mountain • Perry Mason • Rock 'N Roll Rebel • Shot in the Dark.
00248413 Book/Online Audio $19.99

9. ED SHEERAN
The A Team • All of the Stars • Castle on the Hill • Don't • Drunk • Galway Girl • Give Me Love • How Would You Feel (Paean) • I See Fire • Lego House • Make It Rain • Perfect • Photograph • Shape of You • Thinking Out Loud.
00248439 Book/Online Audio $19.99

www.halleonard.com

Prices, contents, and availability subject to change without notice.

HAL·LEONARD® GUITAR PLAY-ALONG

AUDIO ACCESS INCLUDED

INCLUDES TAB

This series will help you play your favorite songs quickly and easily. Just follow the tab and listen to the CD or online audio to hear how the guitar should sound, and then play along using the separate backing tracks. Playback tools are provided for slowing down the tempo without changing pitch and looping challenging parts. The melody and lyrics are included in the book so that you can sing or simply follow along.

85. THE POLICE
00700269................................$16.99

86. BOSTON
00700465................................$16.99

87. ACOUSTIC WOMEN
00700763................................$14.99

88. GRUNGE
00700467................................$16.99

89. REGGAE
00700468................................$15.99

90. CLASSICAL POP
00700469................................$14.99

91. BLUES INSTRUMENTALS
00700505................................$15.99

92. EARLY ROCK INSTRUMENTALS
00700506................................$15.99

93. ROCK INSTRUMENTALS
00700507................................$16.99

94. SLOW BLUES
00700508................................$16.99

95. BLUES CLASSICS
00700509................................$14.99

97. CHRISTMAS CLASSICS
00236542................................$14.99

98. ROCK BAND
00700704................................$14.95

99. ZZ TOP
00700762................................$16.99

100. B.B. KING
00700466................................$16.99

101. SONGS FOR BEGINNERS
00701917................................$14.99

102. CLASSIC PUNK
00700769................................$14.99

103. SWITCHFOOT
00700773................................$16.99

104. DUANE ALLMAN
00700846................................$16.99

105. LATIN
00700939................................$16.99

106. WEEZER
00700958................................$14.99

107. CREAM
00701069................................$16.99

108. THE WHO
00701053................................$16.99

109. STEVE MILLER
00701054................................$16.99

110. SLIDE GUITAR HITS
00701055................................$16.99

111. JOHN MELLENCAMP
00701056................................$14.99

112. QUEEN
00701052................................$16.99

113. JIM CROCE
00701058................................$16.99

114. BON JOVI
00701060................................$16.99

115. JOHNNY CASH
00701070................................$16.99

116. THE VENTURES
00701124................................$16.99

117. BRAD PAISLEY
00701224................................$16.99

118. ERIC JOHNSON
00701353................................$16.99

119. AC/DC CLASSICS
00701356................................$17.99

120. PROGRESSIVE ROCK
00701457................................$14.99

121. U2
00701508................................$16.99

122. CROSBY, STILLS & NASH
00701610................................$16.99

123. LENNON & MCCARTNEY ACOUSTIC
00701614................................$16.99

125. JEFF BECK
00701687................................$16.99

126. BOB MARLEY
00701701................................$16.99

127. 1970S ROCK
00701739................................$16.99

128. 1960S ROCK
00701740................................$14.99

129. MEGADETH
00701741................................$16.99

130. IRON MAIDEN
00701742................................$17.99

131. 1990S ROCK
00701743................................$14.99

132. COUNTRY ROCK
00701757................................$15.99

133. TAYLOR SWIFT
00701894................................$16.99

134. AVENGED SEVENFOLD
00701906................................$16.99

135. MINOR BLUES
00151350................................$17.99

136. GUITAR THEMES
00701922................................$14.99

137. IRISH TUNES
00701966................................$15.99

138. BLUEGRASS CLASSICS
00701967................................$14.99

139. GARY MOORE
00702370................................$16.99

140. MORE STEVIE RAY VAUGHAN
00702396................................$17.99

141. ACOUSTIC HITS
00702401................................$16.99

143. SLASH
00702425................................$19.99

144. DJANGO REINHARDT
00702531................................$16.99

145. DEF LEPPARD
00702532................................$17.99

146. ROBERT JOHNSON
00702533................................$16.99

147. SIMON & GARFUNKEL
14041591................................$16.99

148. BOB DYLAN
14041592................................$16.99

149. AC/DC HITS
14041593................................$17.99

150. ZAKK WYLDE
02501717................................$16.99

151. J.S. BACH
02501730................................$16.99

152. JOE BONAMASSA
02501751................................$19.99

153. RED HOT CHILI PEPPERS
00702990................................$19.99

155. ERIC CLAPTON – FROM THE ALBUM UNPLUGGED
00703085................................$16.99

156. SLAYER
00703770................................$17.99

157. FLEETWOOD MAC
00101382................................$16.99

158. ULTIMATE CHRISTMAS
00101889................................$14.99

159. WES MONTGOMERY
00102593................................$19.99

160. T-BONE WALKER
00102641................................$16.99

161. THE EAGLES – ACOUSTIC
00102659................................$17.99

162. THE EAGLES HITS
00102667................................$17.99

163. PANTERA
00103036................................$17.99

164. VAN HALEN 1986-1995
00110270................................$17.99

165. GREEN DAY
00210343................................$17.99

166. MODERN BLUES
00700764................................$16.99

167. DREAM THEATER
00111938................................$24.99

168. KISS
00113421................................$16.99

169. TAYLOR SWIFT
00115982................................$16.99

170. THREE DAYS GRACE
00117337................................$16.99

171. JAMES BROWN
00117420................................$16.99

173. TRANS-SIBERIAN ORCHESTRA
00119907................................$19.99

174. SCORPIONS
00122119................................$16.99

175. MICHAEL SCHENKER
00122127................................$16.99

176. BLUES BREAKERS WITH JOHN MAYALL & ERIC CLAPTON
00122132................................$19.99

177. ALBERT KING
00123271................................$16.99

178. JASON MRAZ
00124165................................$17.99

179. RAMONES
00127073................................$16.99

180. BRUNO MARS
00129706................................$16.99

181. JACK JOHNSON
00129854................................$16.99

182. SOUNDGARDEN
00138161................................$17.99

183. BUDDY GUY
00138240................................$17.99

184. KENNY WAYNE SHEPHERD
00138258................................$17.99

185. JOE SATRIANI
00139457................................$17.99

186. GRATEFUL DEAD
00139459................................$17.99

187. JOHN DENVER
00140839................................$17.99

188. MÖTLEY CRUE
00141145................................$17.99

189. JOHN MAYER
00144350................................$17.99

191. PINK FLOYD CLASSICS
00146164................................$17.99

192. JUDAS PRIEST
00151352................................$17.99

For complete songlists, visit Hal Leonard online at
www.halleonard.com

Prices, contents, and availability subject to change without notice.

GUITAR *signature licks*

Signature Licks book/audio packs provide a step-by-step breakdown of "right from the record" riffs, licks, and solos so you can jam along with your favorite bands. They contain performance notes and an overview of each artist's or group's style, with note-for-note transcriptions in notes and tab. The CDs or online audio tracks feature full-band demos at both normal and slow speeds.

AC/DC
14041352................$22.99

AEROSMITH 1973-1979
00695106................$22.95

AEROSMITH 1979-1998
00695219................$22.95

DUANE ALLMAN
00696042................$22.99

BEST OF CHET ATKINS
00695752................$22.95

AVENGED SEVENFOLD
00696473................$22.99

BEST OF THE BEATLES FOR ACOUSTIC GUITAR
00695453................$22.99

THE BEATLES BASS
00695283................$22.95

THE BEATLES FAVORITES
00695096................$24.95

THE BEATLES HITS
00695049................$24.95

JEFF BECK
00696427................$22.99

BEST OF GEORGE BENSON
00695418................$22.95

BEST OF BLACK SABBATH
00695249................$22.95

BLUES BREAKERS WITH JOHN MAYALL & ERIC CLAPTON
00696374................$22.99

BON JOVI
00696380................$22.99

ROY BUCHANAN
00696654................$22.99

KENNY BURRELL
00695830................$22.99

BEST OF CHARLIE CHRISTIAN
00695584................$22.95

BEST OF ERIC CLAPTON
00695038................$24.99

ERIC CLAPTON – FROM THE ALBUM UNPLUGGED
00695250................$24.95

BEST OF CREAM
00695251................$22.95

CREEDANCE CLEARWATER REVIVAL
00695924................$22.95

DEEP PURPLE – GREATEST HITS
00695625................$22.99

THE BEST OF DEF LEPPARD
00696516................$22.95

DREAM THEATER
00111943................$24.99

TOMMY EMMANUEL
00696409................$22.99

ESSENTIAL JAZZ GUITAR
00695875................$19.99

FAMOUS ROCK GUITAR SOLOS
00695590................$19.95

FLEETWOOD MAC
00696416................$22.99

BEST OF FOO FIGHTERS
00695481................$24.95

ROBBEN FORD
00695903................$22.95

BEST OF GRANT GREEN
00695747................$22.99

PETER GREEN
00145386................$22.99

THE GUITARS OF ELVIS – 2ND ED.
00174800................$22.99

BEST OF GUNS N' ROSES
00695183................$24.99

THE BEST OF BUDDY GUY
00695186................$22.99

JIM HALL
00695848................$22.99

JIMI HENDRIX
00696560................$24.99

JIMI HENDRIX – VOLUME 2
00695835................$24.95

JOHN LEE HOOKER
00695894................$19.99

BEST OF JAZZ GUITAR
00695586................$24.95

ERIC JOHNSON
00699317................$24.95

ROBERT JOHNSON
00695264................$22.95

BARNEY KESSEL
00696009................$22.99

THE ESSENTIAL ALBERT KING
00695713................$22.95

B.B. KING – BLUES LEGEND
00696039................$22.99

B.B. KING – THE DEFINITIVE COLLECTION
00695635................$22.95

B.B. KING – MASTER BLUESMAN
00699923................$24.99

MARK KNOPFLER
00695178................$24.99

LYNYRD SKYNYRD
00695872................$24.95

THE BEST OF YNGWIE MALMSTEEN
00695669................$22.95

BEST OF PAT MARTINO
00695632................$24.99

MEGADETH
00696421................$22.99

WES MONTGOMERY
00695387................$24.95

BEST OF NIRVANA
00695483................$24.95

VERY BEST OF OZZY OSBOURNE
00695431................$22.99

BRAD PAISLEY
00696379................$22.99

BEST OF JOE PASS
00695730................$22.95

JACO PASTORIUS
00695544................$24.95

TOM PETTY
00696021................$22.99

PINK FLOYD
00103659................$24.99

PINK FLOYD – EARLY CLASSICS
00695566................$22.95

BEST OF QUEEN
00695097................$24.95

RADIOHEAD
00109304................$24.99

BEST OF RAGE AGAINST THE MACHINE
00695480................$24.95

RED HOT CHILI PEPPERS
00695173................$22.95

RED HOT CHILI PEPPERS – GREATEST HITS
00695828................$24.99

JERRY REED
00118236................$22.99

BEST OF DJANGO REINHARDT
00695660................$24.99

BEST OF ROCK 'N' ROLL GUITAR
00695559................$19.95

BEST OF ROCKABILLY GUITAR
00695785................$19.95

BEST OF JOE SATRIANI
00695216................$22.95

SLASH
00696576................$22.99

SLAYER
00121281 Guitar $22.99

THE BEST OF SOUL GUITAR
00695703................$19.95

BEST OF SOUTHERN ROCK
00695560................$19.95

STEELY DAN
00696015................$22.99

MIKE STERN
00695800................$24.99

BEST OF SURF GUITAR
00695822................$19.99

STEVE VAI
00673247................$22.95

STEVE VAI – ALIEN LOVE SECRETS: THE NAKED VAMPS
00695223................$22.95

STEVE VAI – FIRE GARDEN: THE NAKED VAMPS
00695166................$22.95

STEVE VAI – THE ULTRA ZONE: NAKED VAMPS
00695684................$22.95

VAN HALEN
00110227................$24.99

STEVIE RAY VAUGHAN – 2ND ED.
00699316................$24.95

THE GUITAR STYLE OF STEVIE RAY VAUGHAN
00695155................$24.95

BEST OF THE VENTURES
00695772................$19.95

THE WHO – 2ND ED.
00695561................$22.95

JOHNNY WINTER
00695951................$22.99

YES
00113120................$22.99

NEIL YOUNG – GREATEST HITS
00695988................$22.99

BEST OF ZZ TOP
00695738................$24.95

HAL•LEONARD®

www.halleonard.com

COMPLETE DESCRIPTIONS AND SONGLISTS ONLINE!

Prices, contents and availability subject to change without notice.

0817